"YOUR COUNTRY NEEDS YOU"

THE SECRET HISTORY
OF THE
PROPAGANDA POSTER

JAMES TAYLOR

Saraband 🌀

To Berenice Webb

Published by Saraband
Suite 202, 98 Woodlands Road
Glasgow, G3 6HB, Scotland
www.saraband.net

ISBN: 978-188735497-4
ebook: 978-190864311-7

Publisher: Sara Hunt
Editor: Craig Hillsley
Graphic design: Jo Morley
Cover design: Chloe van Grieken
Production assistant: Emily Ferro

1 3 5 7 9 10 8 6 4 2

CONTENTS

INTRODUCTION

THIS BOOK COINCIDES with the global centenary commemorations of World War I and it reveals, for the first time, the true story and full extent of the vital role played by the art and design of recruitment posters in the war – not just in the UK, but around the world in Europe, Australia, Canada, India, South Africa and the USA. The posters were particularly important during the initial stages of the conflict, when they were devised as part of a wide-ranging campaign to recruit the millions of men needed for frontline action. Today, one poster above all others is recollected by name: YOUR COUNTRY NEEDS YOU. It is a poster that we all feel we know so well, but do we really?

There is no doubting the enduring influence of the striking, arm-stretching and finger-pointing cartoon of Lord Kitchener first created by the British-born commercial artist Alfred Leete as the cover for *London Opinion* magazine on 5th September 1914. The original artwork for this cartoon was acquired by the Imperial War Museum in 1917 and has ever since been mistakenly assimilated into the minds of millions as being one and the same as an imagined recruitment poster bearing the same slogan with mass appeal. But was this

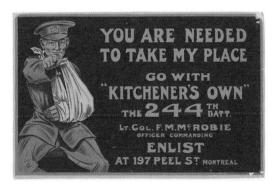

poster really as popular as people now think? There is certainly evidence that the image of the cartoon – as opposed to the poster – was very popular. For example, *London Opinion*, which sold more than a quarter of a million copies a week in the early months of the war, issued reproductions of the cartoon on fine art paper. Postcards bearing the image are also thought to have appeared in order to aid recruitment.

The popularity and success of the Kitchener cartoon lies in its combination of an easy-to-remember slogan and a simplistic and adaptable design that derived from commercial advertising pre-dating the war. However, there is no conclusive evidence to support the claims made by many historians that a poster version of Leete's cartoon was the most popular and effective official design of the war. A list of the official posters in order of popularity has been compiled here and Leete is conspicuous by his absence. Leete's poster was published privately and no records survive of the precise numbers printed.

As well as examining the story of Leete's Kitchener image, this book delves into the remarkable life and achievements of Leete himself, and explores the influence of cartoonist contemporaries such as Bruce Bairnsfather (creator of 'Old Bill') and John Hassall

(SKEGNESS IS SO BRACING), alongside the colourful and controversial world of the brilliant American artist, cartoonist and illustrator James Montgomery Flagg. In 1917, Flagg adapted Leete's design for his celebrated poster depicting Uncle Sam. Entitled I WANT YOU FOR U.S. ARMY, it is arguably the most familiar image in the USA after the 'Stars and Stripes' national flag.

The designs of both Leete and Flagg still resonate powerfully today and have been used for many diverse campaigns for economic, educational, financial, military and political purposes during World War II and in the following decades up to the present day. They have become design icons.

Left: Canadian poster based on the Kitchener image.
Across: Downing Street office during World War I.
Below: James Montgomery Flagg's Uncle Sam poster.

CHAPTER 1

'YOUR COUNTRY NEEDS YOU'

SEPARATING FACT FROM FICTION

O N A SMALL HILL in the seaside town of Weston-super-Mare is the striking Art Deco grave of the British-born artist, cartoonist and illustrator Alfred Leete (28th August 1882 – 17th June 1933), the man who created what is now widely regarded to be one of the world's most familiar and popular poster designs. It is generally known, although mistakenly so, by the title YOUR COUNTRY NEEDS YOU and depicts the steely stare, out-stretched arm and accusing pointing finger of Lord Kitchener, exhorting the viewer to enlist and do their bit for their country.

Kitchener played a crucial role during World War I as Secretary of State for War; and tradi-tionally it is believed that through the combina-tion of Leete's forceful and eye-catching image and Kitchener's military prowess and popularity this poster design was instrumental in raising the armies of millions of men for frontline duty until conscription was introduced in 1916.

Today, Leete's KITCHENER design can be found emblazoned on aprons, bookmarks, fridge magnets, mouse mats, mugs, note-books, oven gloves, postcards, posters, towels and T-shirts. However, an in-depth examina-tion of the evidence relating to the creation of this poster, its printing, posting and popularity during the war reveals alternative and surpris-ing stories.

A privately printed poster, not an official design

At the outset of World War I, the Parliamentary Recruiting Committee (PRC) was established in order to enlist men for the fighting services. Headquartered in London, the PRC was able to employ a variety of means to achieve this goal, including the production and distribution of posters. Leete's design, however, was not for-mally part of that official organisation. It was printed privately. The poster was actually only one of more than two hundred official and pri-vate recruitment posters produced during the war, with the PRC producing the lion's share: some 164 designs.[1]

There are two main reasons why Leete's poster could not have been officially produced. Dr Nicholas Hiley, Head of the British Cartoon Archive at the Templeman Library, University of Kent, has succinctly outlined them: 'Not only did it first appear in September 1914 when the PRC was still committed to letterpress posters, but it also employed a personal appeal that ran counter to the official tradition of recruiting in the name of the King.'[2]

Alfred Leete's original KITCHENER artwork for the so-called YOUR COUNTRY NEEDS YOU

poster, although this was not its original purpose, now forms part of the collections of the
Imperial War Museum (IWM) in London,
kindly donated by Leete himself. It had been for-
mally acquired by mid-October 1917, according
to Richard Slocombe, the current Senior Curator
of Art at the IWM. The first curator responsible
for acquiring and cataloguing the visual material during the war period was Mr L.R. Bradley.
Slocombe has identified a letter dated 18th
October 1917 in which Bradley thanks Leete
for his 'gift of five original drawings, including
the original of the famous Kitchener drawing'.
Leete had suggested to Bradley that the artwork
be returned if it was felt to be too damaged for
the IWM collections – there is a noticeable tear
upper centre of the artwork and some minor
damage caused by folding. Fortunately, the
IWM retained the drawing (see page 8).

The IWM was established by the War
Cabinet on 5th March 1917 and its first home
was at the Crystal Palace. The museum was
opened by King George V on 9th June 1920
when the first Chairman, Sir Alfred Mond,
British MP, financier, industrialist and
founder of Imperial Chemical Industries
(ICI), addressed the King saying that 'it was
hoped to make the museum so complete that
everyone who took part in the war, however
obscurely, would find therein an example or
illustration of the sacrifice he or she made'
and that the museum 'was not a monument
of military glory, but a record of toil and
sacrifice'.[3] However, there is no evidence to
confirm that Leete's 'famous Kitchener drawing' was on display in the museum at this time.

'Your Country Needs YOU' as a magazine cover

The design was not originally created as a
poster but rather as artwork for a war cartoon
for *London Opinion* magazine that featured
on the cover of the 5th September 1914 edition with the caption 'Your Country Needs
YOU'. This black and white magazine had
been established more than a decade earlier
on 26th December 1903 as 'A popular paper
full of Original Articles, Essays and Reviews,
with Tales, Sketches and Illustrations' and was
published at 36, Southampton Street, Strand,

Across: Alfred Leete.

Right: Poster advertising the Great War Exhibition
at Crystal Palace.

Above: The Kitchener cartoon's first appearance on the cover of *London Opinion*.

London. Leete excelled as a cartoonist and commercial illustrator and had a long and rewarding relationship with this magazine. He had created many cover designs and cartoons for the magazine prior to his LORD KITCHENER design and in fact he was still contributing cartoons up until his death in 1933.

An example of the news-stand poster incorporating Leete's Kitchener cartoon and promoting the sale of the *London Opinion* issue of 5th September 1914 is now in the collections of the Library of Congress in the USA. As its advertorial function determined, the poster featured the name of the magazine prominently at the top of the poster and towards the bottom it was repeated in smaller type, as well as indicating the price of '1d' (one penny). It combined commercial self-promotion with a patriotism that captured the mood of the war at that time.

During the early summer of 1914, *London Opinion* boasted a weekly circulation of almost 300,000. The last edition in May sold 295,000 copies, although circulation and advertising slumped in the first weeks of the war. However, it picked up. In *The Street of Ink, an Intimate History of Journalism*, published in 1917, author Henry Simonis noted that from the beginning of the war '…things gradually mended, and then improved, and then boomed, until to-day circulation and advertising, revenue and turnover are all at records'.

The weekly circulation figures printed within individual issues of *London Opinion* indicate that numbers were still impressive by modern standards. In the week prior to the publication of Leete's Kitchener cartoon cover, the circulation was 251,000, and in the edition when the cartoon made its first appearance the number had increased to 257,000. In the following two issues the figures also showed an upward trend, increasing to 265,000 and then 270,000.

Shortly after Britain declared war against Germany on 4th August 1914, the editor of *London Opinion* claimed it had been bombarded with requests for copies of their illustrations and cartoons. An advertorial of 12th September 1914 announced that 'The War Cartoons Appearing in *London Opinion* are being reproduced by many of the leading newspapers in the kingdom. At the request of many readers the following pictures have already been printed on fine art paper, suitable for framing.'

They included one work by the Glasgow-born artist, illustrator and cartoonist

Alexander Stuart Boyd (1854–1930) and four by Welshman Bert Thomas (1883–1966), who was famous for his cartoon-poster of a grinning Cockney Tommy lighting a pipe with the caption 'Arf a 'Mo', Kaiser!' It appeared in the *Weekly Dispatch* of 11th November 1914 as part of the paper's tobacco-for-troops fund, which raised an estimated £250,000. Leete provided five works, the largest number, including Your Country Needs YOU. His other popular cartoons were listed as: 'Yah! [sic] I will make meinself bigger or burst' (15th August), 'Our Jack, Britain's Trump Card' (15th August), 'Got Him!' (22nd August) and 'He didn't know it was loaded' (29th August). They were offered for sale 'post free for Sixpence each'.

JA! I WILL MAKE MEINSELF BIGGER OR BURST

The fine art paper printing of Your Country Needs YOU was the first time this particular design was produced independently of the magazine, but it was specifically created as a small-scale souvenir for private enjoyment rather than as a poster in the strict sense of the word.

The 'Golden Age' of the postcard

On 12th September 1914, another *London Opinion* advertorial stated that 'We are getting numerous applications from various recruiting organisations for postcards reproducing last week's LO cover – the Kitchener head, "Your

Above: 'Tobacco-for-troops' fundraising cartoon.
Left: Satirical postcard by Leete for *London Opinion*.

News-stand poster advertising the 5th September 1914 edition of *London Opinion*. Printed by the Victoria House Printing Co. Ltd. Across: Bassano's photograph x96369 of Kitchener, 1900, and a postcard 'adapting' Leete's design, printed by the Regent Publishing Co. Ltd., September 1914.

Country Needs YOU" – in colour. To aid in recruiting we will supply these at the rate of 1s. 4d a 100. Post free.' These postcards may well have been produced, but locating examples in public or private collections remains an ongoing challenge.

In 'Round The Town', a regular feature of *London Opinion* that appeared in the issue of 26th September 1914, it was announced that 'A certain publishing firm has just issued a portrait of Lord Kitchener with finger pointing out of the picture, on which are the words 'YOU Are The Man I Want'. I seem to have seen something like this before – in a previous existence, probably!' This ironic statement refers to the colour postcard depicting Lord Kitchener in a red uniform, without his hat, with outstretched arm and pointing finger. It was captioned 'YOU

Are The Man I Want'. An example was on display in the former First World War Galleries of the Imperial War Museum (IWM reference: K50155). There is another example in the Victoria and Albert Museum.

Although *London Opinion* would contract independent printer-publishers to produce postcards on its behalf, there would invariably be a printed credit line indicating the original source as '*London Opinion*'. However, in this instance it appears that the creation and ownership of the design 'YOU Are The Man I Want' lies elsewhere. The only details on the card are: 'The WAR Series, No.1851, Printed in England. The Regent Publishing Co., Ltd, London, N.W.1 (ALL BRITISH) Photo by Bassano.'

The Regent Publishing Co. was based in Euston Road, London, from 1905 until 1925

and issued cards of various subjects, including actors and royalty and especially views of London often in the form of original hand-coloured photographs. During the war the market for cards was fiercely competitive and it is therefore likely, in light of the ironic comment, that this company had cheekily adapted Leete's cartoon and devised a new slogan so as to claim it as one of their own postcard designs. That said, the company had been careful to acknowledge the photographic source of Lord Kitchener as deriving from Alexander Bassano.

Bassano created some of the most sought-after photographic portraits of Kitchener, although none of them depicted him with an outstretched arm and accusing finger. Leete had transformed the same photographic source (outlined in more detail later in this chapter) into his memorable cartoon, although he made no reference to Bassano. Leete probably believed that as his pictorial design was so radically different to the conventional portrait image of Kitchener, there was no need. He was the first to combine the finger-pointing format with a prominent British personality.

Another advert promoting the war cartoons printed on fine art paper appeared in the 26th September issue of *London Opinion*, which had a cover cartoon by Leete lampooning Austria with the caption 'Serves Me Right. I Started It'. The war cartoons included 'Your Country Needs YOU', with an additional design by Leete, entitled 'The Goal is Berlin', which first featured in the 12th September edition. Shorter adverts promoting these war cartoons also appeared in October and November editions.

Details of the production of additional postcards were also announced by the editor of

Above: Alexander Bassano.

Across: Soldier of the Black Watch (Royal Highlanders) in France. This poster was turned into a wartime postcard.

London Opinion on 31st October 1914: 'Owing to the great popularity of the "L.O" war cartoons, as shown by the many applications for special pulls on art paper, arrangements have now been completed with Messrs. Lawrence and Jellicoe for a selection to be reproduced in the form of coloured post-cards. Look out for these at your stationer's.'

In Peter Doyle's *British Postcards of the First World War* (Shire Publications, 2010), he noted that 'During the years 1914–18, at the height of its "Golden Age", the postcard was ubiquitous;

worldwide in use and popularity. Postcards were sent (and collected avidly) by civilian and soldier alike, and were to cross all social boundaries, from the lowliest private soldier to the loftiest general.'

Receiving post was one of the highlights of the arduous day-to-day life on the Western Front. Sorting and distribution depots were located in several areas of northern France and millions of items, including postcards, were handled during the war. The British Post Office was responsible for censoring post from the troops and this took place at Le Havre and later Boulogne. Censorship was necessary to catch spies and prevent troops from accidentally revealing vital information to the enemy, and also to stop the spread of outbreaks of low morale.

Today, one prominent website promoting the history of World War I postcards – www.worldwar1postcards.com – has neatly summarised their popularity: 'The newsagents W.H. Smith displayed numerous categories of war-related cards in the postcard racks of its 2,000 shops. In addition, booksellers, cinemas, corner shops, stationary stores, public houses, haberdashery stores, post offices and branches of Boots the Chemist and numerous other commercial outlets sold them. By 1915, "war cards" were also displayed and offered for sale in the thousands of Y.M.C.A. canteens in military training camps at home and on the Western Front and elsewhere.'

That picture-postcards are now treated seriously by art curators and galleries is evident in a major exhibition, entitled *The Postcard Age*, held at the Museum of Fine Arts in Boston, USA (October 2012 – April 2013). The museum's marketing department has outlined their importance: 'In the decades around 1900, postcards were Twitter, e-mail, Flickr and Facebook, all wrapped into one. A postcard craze swept the world as billions of cards were bought and mailed, or just pasted in albums. Four hundred cards by a wide variety of artists and publishers from throughout Europe and the Americas are arranged by theme (including World War I). The result is a vivid picture of the cares and concerns of the age and a tempting sampler of the artistic and historical roles found in this private archive, the lifetime work of Leonard A. Lauder (part of the Estée Lauder family company) and a promised gift to the museum.' The Regent Publishing Co. postcard depicting Lord Kitchener captioned 'YOU Are The Man I Want' featured in this exhibition.

On 21st November 1914, *London Opinion* announced that '…some of the most popular of these drawings [war cartoons] are now published in a series of Twelve Postcards Printed in Colour. The cards may be purchased at any bookstall or newsagent etc Price 1d each or direct from Lawrence & Jellicoe, Henrietta Street, W.C. [Covent Garden].' By Christmas time the number of retailers selling them had been expanded to meet the demand. The magazine issue of 26th December 1914 stated that 'postcards of war cartoons were now available from W. H. Smith and Son and J. Beagles & Co Ltd'.

On 2nd December 1914, the commentator in 'Round The Town' noted: 'I have been looking through the *London Opinion* coloured War postcards, published by Messrs. Lawrence and Jellicoe of Henrietta Street and find it very difficult to say which are likely to prove the more popular. Perhaps, if I plump for "The Iron Cross – A German Honour that has become

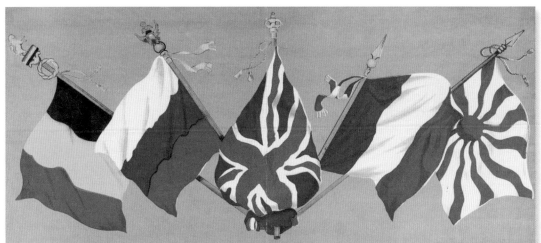

DON'T IMAGINE YOU ARE NOT WANTED

EVERY MAN between 19 and 38 years of age is WANTED!

Ex-Soldiers up to 45 years of age

"YOUR COUNTRY NEEDS YOU"

MEN CAN ENLIST IN THE NEW ARMY FOR THE DURATION OF THE WAR

RATE OF PAY: Lowest Scale 7s. per week with Food, Clothing &c., in addition

1. **Separation Allowance for Wives and Children of Married Men when separated from their Families** (inclusive of the allotment required from the Soldier's pay of a maximum of 6d. a day in the case of a private)

For a Wife **without** Children	-	12s. 6d. per week
For Wife with One Child	-	15s. 0d. per week
For Wife with Two Children	-	17s. 6d. per week
For Wife with Three Children	-	20s. 0d. per week
For Wife with Four Children	-	22s. 0d. per week

and so on, with an addition of 2s. for each additional child.
Motherless children 3s. a week each, exclusive of allotment from Soldier's pay

2. **Separation Allowance for Dependants of Unmarried Men.**

Provided the Soldier does his share, the Government will assist liberally in keeping up, within the limits of Separation Allowance for Families, any regular contribution made before enlistment by unmarried Soldiers or Widowers to other dependants such as mothers, fathers, sisters, etc.

**YOUR COUNTRY IS STILL CALLING.
FIGHTING MEN! FALL IN!!**

Full Particulars can be obtained at any Recruiting Office or Post Office.

Nº 0200
DAVID ALLEN & SONS Ld
HARROW
LONDON

The only known recruitment poster to feature the words 'Your Country Needs YOU' and Leete's Kitchener image. Poster printed and designed by David Allen and Sons.

a Shame" by Bert Thomas and "Our Jack of Trumps" by Alfred Leete I shall not be so wide of the mark.' Leete's humorous cartoon 'Our Jack, Britain's Trump Card' depicted a sailor in the form of a playing card with the name 'Invincible' around his hat.

The 'BRITONS – Wants YOU' poster

In September 1914, Leete's cartoon of Kitchener had featured for the first time in a propaganda poster printed by the Victoria House Printing Co. Ltd., Tudor St, London. The actual caption of the poster was not 'Your Country Needs YOU' but instead 'BRITONS – [Lord Kitchener] Wants YOU – Join Your Country's Army!' with the words 'God Save The King' printed below, and beneath that 'Reproduced by permission of *London Opinion*'. This credit line was specifically designed to promote the magazine with authority, however some writers have misconstrued the meaning as implying that the poster was printed on behalf of another organisation, an official one. Until fairly recently a printing company called 'Victoria House...' was still trading, although no records of their poster productions during the war period have been traced.[4]

As a weekly publication, *London Opinion* was geared up to turn out printed matter rapidly, and although the BRITONS – WANTS YOU poster was not actually dated, it is widely believed that it was issued before the end of September 1914.

A second more elaborate and larger recruitment poster was printed in November 1914, this time by the company David Allen and

Sons Ltd., which was active from the late 1850s to 1965. It was adorned with national flags and featured the original magazine cover slogan 'Your Country Needs YOU' with details of rates of pay and other information, including the additional words 'Your Country Is Still Calling. Fighting Men! Fall In!!'

This variant is the only known example of this period to combine the slogan 'Your Country Needs YOU' with Leete's wartime cartoon of Kitchener. However, this elaborate, colourful version combined too many descriptive and pictorial elements, making the overall effect overblown. The Kitchener image and accompanying slogan is small in comparison to the *London Opinion* poster and to an extent it is smothered by the surrounding design scheme. There is no evidence that this variant was a popular or effective poster.

The main factories and offices of David Allen and Sons were in Harrow, Middlesex and in Belfast. They also had offices in Dublin, Glasgow, Liverpool and London in Fleet Street. No doubt aided by this wide-ranging business network, they worked extensively for the PRC. In fact around a quarter of the PRC posters were contracted to David Allen and Sons. The following companies were also utilised: Chorley and Pickersgill; Hazell, Watson and Viney; Johnson, Riddell and Company; and Roberts and Leete among others. However, the David Allen poster featuring Leete's Kitchener cartoon was not commissioned by the PRC, but produced privately. The poster had no artist's signature and the overall design of the poster incorporating Leete's Kitchener cartoon as a central feature may well have been the work of John Hassall, who worked on special projects for David Allen and Sons,

Only three examples of the signed *London Opinion* poster, measuring 74.5 x 50.9cm, are known to exist.

or alternatively one of their in-house artists, rather than Leete himself.[5]

In his book *The History of a Family Firm, 1857–1957* (John Murray, 1957), W.E.D. Allen mentioned several notable artists who were managed from the company's Belfast office during World War I: 'The Studio was controlled by an artist named A.B. White, whose habit was to suck constantly sulphur tablets. Whether he did this for health's sake or because he liked them was never known. The artists used by Allens in the main office in Belfast were the pick of the bunch. They included Pat Kinsalla, a big buoyant, plump Irishman with a wonderful sense of colour and personality to match. Albert Morrow, Will True, Stewart Browne, Robert Montgomery, A. Tugwell, T.E. Stephens (now a very famous artist in the USA), Reg Rigby (who did the celebrated posters for The Follies, that unique Pierrot combination), Barribal (who created a wonderful girl – the model for which was his beautiful wife), Gilbert Holliday, David Wilson and W. Piffard. Also a fine artist named Cunio [Terence Cuneo]. And Allens would also commission John Hassall and others of eminence for special jobs.'

In *Keep the Home Fires Burning* (Allen Lane, 1977), Cate Haste asserted that 'Though most of the PRC posters did not reflect modern developments in design, there was one exception, their first and most famous, the Lord Kitchener poster. The design, by Alfred Leete, first appeared on the front cover of the London weekly magazine *London Opinion* on 15th September 1914 [a text error that should read 5th September 1914]. The Committee [PRC] took it over and added "God Save the King" to Kitchener's face. The original spawned numerous variations. It was the most

successful poster of the war, and it established Kitchener's image as the embodiment of the nation's resolution and strength. He recalled Britain's imperial victories. Even government leaders who later doubted his capacity to manage the war paid tribute to the success his image had in inspiring confidence at the beginning. Miss Elizabeth Asquith called Kitchener himself "The Great Poster".'

Haste's publication is thought-provoking, however, the aforementioned extract contains unsubstantiated claims. All the PRC posters bear details indicating that they were officially endorsed, with each poster design being assigned a unique number, from 1 to 164. Although David Allen and Sons was one of the officially approved printers, as previously mentioned, this alone does not prove that this poster was an official PRC design. In fact, no PRC endorsements can be found on any of posters featuring Leete's cartoon of Kitchener.

The military historian Peter Simkins noted in *Kitchener's Army: The Raising of the New Armies 1914–1916* (Manchester University Press, 1988) that 'The Parliamentary Recruiting Committee also obtained permission to use the design [Leete's Lord Kitchener cartoon] with a slightly amended text which included at Kitchener's insistence the words "God Save the King".' In this referenced publication there is no indication of the source for his assertion, although it is reminiscent of Haste.

Conclusive evidence of the private printing of the BRITONS – WANTS YOU poster can be found within the pages of *London Opinion* itself. In the 19th December 1914 issue, it was

Across: Official poster using Leete's slogan
(see page 69).

Follow me!

Published by the PARLIAMENTARY RECRUITING COMMITTEE, London.   Poster No. 11.   W. 8322   H.M. 12/14

YOUR COUNTRY
NEEDS YOU

Printed by HILL, SIFFKEN & Co. (L.P.A. Ltd.), Grafton Works, London, N.

noted that 'The famous Kitchener recruiting poster, issued by *London Opinion*, is doing good work in every part of the Empire, and not least in Ontario, to judge from a note received by the editor from the town of Hamilton, in which the writer (a former employee on the Great Central Railway at Wendover) says: "The 13th and the 91st Regiments come by our house as they go to the drill ground. We have put the poster in the window, and as they march by they all glance at it, while some salute it."'

The *London Opinion* editor's words 'The famous Kitchener recruiting poster' are of course linked to promoting the magazine itself. Evidence presented in this book reveals the remarkable popularity of the Kitchener cartoon, but the same cannot be said unequivocally about the poster. In addition to Canada there is only one other traceable record of the BRITONS – Wants YOU poster being in circulation within the British Empire before the end of the war. In Australia, the poster was acquired by the State Library of Victoria, Melbourne, on 30th March 1918, and *London Opinion* was almost certainly responsible for dispatching it. Although it is noted within the museum's acquisition file that it was part of a collection donated by the Great Britain Parliamentary Recruiting Committee (a subsequent batch of posters was also donated by the Commonwealth Recruiting Committee, Sydney) the obvious explanation is that the *London Opinion* design was swept up with the official posters without any distinction being made in terms of their official or private status.

It is also possible that there was some approval by the PRC (albeit unofficial) of the privately printed recruitment posters. In some instances perhaps the PRC and related governmental services might have helped with their transportation, distribution and posting abroad, and possibly within Britain too – after all, they were serving the same purpose. However, in the absence of documentary evidence such claims remain conjecture.

Contrasting recollections of 'Your Country Needs YOU'

The effectiveness and popularity of the BRITONS – Wants YOU poster around the world is difficult to gauge, as evidence from independent and unbiased sources of the poster being a celebrated design is not generally available. In most cases the claims of having seen it are usually muddled, as the recollections have been made long after the end of the war.

The poster might have been seen by some printing and publishing companies, especially those located in or near London, where it was relatively easy for *London Opinion* to distribute them. There may well have been some sightings of Leete's cartoon in postcards, reproductions on fine art paper or possibly within newspapers, however, it is far more likely that the aforementioned companies, in Britain and abroad, would have been familiar with it through direct purchase of *London Opinion*.

Company directors and managers along with their printers, artists and cartoonists would scour the pages of magazines for ideas and inspiration, as well as to identify prospective corporate clients by noting carefully the diverse range of advertisements. The directness of Leete's Lord Kitchener cartoon cover of 5th September 1914 and the simplicity of the slogan would certainly have caught their attention. The actual size of this magazine was around 29.5 x 20.5 cm (almost exactly the same size as an A4 piece of paper) and it contained less than thirty thin pages, making it easy to store as a source of reference. This slim magazine priced at one penny punched well above its weight in terms of influence and popularity.

Some of the war veterans recalling their experiences many years later have quite understandably muddled memories about what they actually saw, and what influenced them in terms of signing up. A good example featured in a series of TV programmes called *Lost Heroes of World War One*, broadcast on Channel 5 in the UK. The episode *The Call to Arms* on 7th November 2011 featured Robert 'Robbie' Burns, who joined the 7th Queen's Own Cameron Highlanders. He served on the Western Front from 1915, fought at the Battle of Loos and was wounded at the Somme in 1916. 'Robbie' said: 'Everywhere you went in Glasgow there were great big posters up with Kitchener with his finger pointing at you. No matter where you were, this finger seemed to be pointing at you, "Your King and Country Needs You".'

No recorded posters are known that feature Leete's Kitchener design

Right: The 'Call to Arms' that first appeared in *The Times*.

with the slogan 'Your King and Country Needs You'. However, it is known that advertisements featured in many magazines and national newspapers across Britain with a similar slogan. On 7th August 1914, *The Times*, owned by Lord Northcliffe, printed the official 'Call to Arms', one of many official messages issued by the government on behalf of the King, the Prime Minister and Lord Kitchener. It read: 'Your King & Country Need You. A Call To Arms. An addition of 100,000 MEN to His Majesty's Regular Army is immediately necessary in the present grave National Emergency. Lord Kitchener is confident that this appeal will be at once responded to by all those who have the safety of our Empire at heart.' The advertisement also included the terms of service, details of how to join and ended with the words 'God Save The King'.

A second advertisement appeal for an additional 100,000 men also appeared in *The Times* on 28th August. These letterpress advertisements, notices and posters were produced under the guiding hand and supervision of Hedley Francis Le Bas, and YOUR KING AND COUNTRY NEED YOU was produced by the Caxton Publishing Company, a business that he had established in 1899.

Le Bas was a Jerseyman, former soldier and salesman for the Manchester publishers Blackie and Son. He became an influential paid adviser to the government on advertising prior to and during the war. The actual copy was created by his Advertising Manager, Eric Field, who recalled that 'He [Le Bas] swore me to secrecy, told me that war was imminent and that the moment it broke out we have to start advertising at once… That night I worked out a draft schedule and wrote an advertisement headed "Your King and Country Need You" with the inevitable coat of arms at the top.'[6]

Hedley Francis Le Bas.

Within the pages of *London Opinion* on 15th August 1914, there was also a full-page advert that carried one of the official recruitment slogans: 'Your King and Country Need You… Join the Army to-day!' Variants of these letterpress advertisements were later turned into letterpress and pictorial posters issued by the PRC. Leete adapted this topical official slogan for his own war cartoon, and its similarity probably explains why people get confused today about which slogan relates to which poster design. Judging from 'Robbie's' detailed description he may have seen a poster. The *Evening Telegraph* of Dundee noted on 26th April 1915 in 'The Appeal of the Poster' that 'It is impossible to escape the war posters… Lord Kitchener bars the way with a terrible look and menacing finger.' Robbie has fused together in his mind the image and slogan from separate sources.

Several recruitment slogans were turned into marching ballads and popular songs, notably in Britain, Australia and Canada. Prominent among them were: 'Your King and Country Need You', written and composed by Paul Pelham, W.H. Wallis and Fred Elton; 'Your Country Needs YOU Now' by A.L. Dubin, Rennie Cormack and Geo. B. McConnell; 'The Call to Arms' by Jack Thomson; and 'Your King & Country Want You', written in 1914 by the librettist and songwriter Paul Alfred Rubens (1875–1917). It featured the line 'For your King and your Country both need you so'. Rubens contributed to and created several popular Edwardian musical comedies that included *Mr Popple (of Ippleton)* in 1905, *The Dairymaid* (1906), *Miss Hook of Holland* (1907) and *The Sunshine Girl* (1912). The singer Helen Clark and the veteran music hall star Vesta Tilley helped to popularise 'Your King & Country Want You' and it was often performed at recruitment rallies, where Tilley would dress up as a soldier. She earned the nickname of 'Britain's best recruiting sergeant'. They also sang *Pack Up Your Troubles in Your Old Kit-Bag, and Smile, Smile, Smile*, the marching song written by George Henry Powell and published in 1915.

Your King & Country Want You
We've watched you playing cricket
and every kind of game,
At football, golf and polo
you men have made your name,
But now your country calls you
to play your part in war,
And no matter what befalls you

we shall love you all the more,
So come and join the forces
as your fathers did before.

Oh, we don't want to lose you
but we think you ought to go;
For your King and your Country
both need you so.
We shall want you and miss you
but with all our might and main,
We shall cheer you, thank you, kiss you
when you come back again.

YOUR KING AND COUNTRY NEED YOU was also parodied in poetical form in *London Opinion* on 31st October 1914 in 'The Peep Show' feature, captioned 'At The Front'. ('The food supplies and commissariat arrangements at the front are excellent' – extract from a soldier's letter.)

"Your King and Country Need You!"
You Know the message pat;
"Your King and Country feed you!"
There's comfort too, in that.

Some people have certainly claimed that they saw posters featuring Leete's cartoon of Kitchener, however, the number of authentic sightings is remarkably small in relation to its current extraordinary reputation. The Italian historian Carlo Ginzburg presented three witnesses.[7] The first was Michael MacDonagh, a journalist for *The Times* and author of *In London during the Great War – the diary of a journalist*, published in 1935. Writing about a scene in London on 3rd January 1915, he observed: 'Posters appealing to recruits are to be seen on every hoarding, in most shop windows, in omnibuses, tramcars and commercial

Bassano studio photograph of Kitchener, 1910.

vans. The great base of Nelson's Pillar [Nelson's Column in Trafalgar Square, London] is covered with them. Their number and variety are remarkable. Everywhere Lord Kitchener sternly points a monstrously big finger, exclaiming "I Want You".

However, the slogan MacDonagh recalled is not one attributable to Leete, but it is reminiscent of the slogan associated with James Montgomery Flagg's well-known propaganda poster I WANT YOU FOR U.S. ARMY of 1917, which was adapted from Leete's war cartoon (see Chapter 4).

The second witness was the English writer Sir Francis Osbert Sacheverell Sitwell, 5th Baronet, (1892–1969). His elder sister was Dame Edith Louisa Sitwell and his younger brother was Sir Sacheverell Sitwell; and like them he devoted his entire life to art and literature. Osbert Sitwell's observations on seeing Kitchener in the flesh, and the recruitment

EVERYONE SHOULD DO HIS BIT

ENLIST NOW

poster that featured him, featured in one part of the writer's autobiography, entitled *Great Morning – Being the Third Volume of Left Hand, Right Hand* (Macmillan, 1948). They are conveyed in his characteristically florid style: 'As the nights of 1914 wore on, their splendour increased. There was no sign of anything amiss, no sudden chilling of the blood, unless it were at the single glimpse I obtained of Lord Kitchener, sitting like a pagod in flowers and exotic leaves.'

Sitwell continued: 'With an altogether squareness and solidity, [Kitchener] sat there as if he were a god, slightly gone to seed perhaps, but waiting confidently for his earthly dominion to disclose itself... a slightly unfocused glance which seemed almost in its fixity to possess a power of divination… And you could, in the mind's eye, see his image set up as that of an English god, by natives in different points of the Empire which he had helped to create and support, precisely as the Roman Emperors had formerly been worshiped. Within a few months' time, when from every hoarding vast posters showed Lord Kitchener pointing into perspectives in space, so steadily perceived, if focused with uncertainty, and below, the caption "He wants YOU!" I often thought of that square figure.' It is odd how this historian omitted the word 'BRITONS' from the actual slogan used in the *London Opinion* poster.

The third witness was Mont Abbott, who worked as a farmhand in Oxfordshire during the war. His recollections of the time were compiled and edited by Sheila Stewart from taped interviews in *Lifting the Latch: A Life on the Land, based on the Life of Mont Abbott of Enstone Oxfordshire* (Oxford University Press, 1987). In that book, Mont Abbott said: 'The gwoost [ghost] of Kitchener had been fading [*sic*] his finger at me for some time on they [*sic*] washed-out posters outside the Post-Office, "Your King and Country Need You". Being up to my eyes the last few years in "Rosy's rump", lone calves, mad bulls, and hungry horses out at Fulwell I hadn't had time to list [*sic*] at Kitchener. But by 1918 the old gwoost were cropping up afresh, pointing at me from barn doors and tree trunks "Your King and Country Need You". This caption derives from the official 'Call to Arms' and recalls the marching ballads and songs.

He continued: 'The Germans were hammering yet again at our exhausted lads in the fifth army, 90,000 of our men and 1,300 of our guns taken at Lys. I'd be sixteen in July. I only hoped the lads could hold out till I got there.'

Mont Abbott went on to explain: 'On my sixteenth birthday, 16th July 1918, I went to enlist with four other bwoys [*sic*] from our Enstone… our old school boss, Mr Glover… were proud to see his "new men", shook hands with each of us and directed us straightaway to the new recruiting station office that had opened up in St Giles, Oxford.'

Although Mont Abbott recalled an image of Kitchener on posters, it is not entirely clear if it really was the Leete design. He made one reference to Kitchener 'fading his finger', however, the words 'pointing at me' might not necessarily refer to Kitchener's pointing finger, but rather that the number of the posters in his locality, over time, had simply caught Abbot's attention. The slogan certainly

Across: Baron Low's poster of recruitment posters within a poster.

Montreal recruiting station.

derives from one of the official messages from the King that by this time would have featured on many thousands of posters. The fact that Mont Abbott was still seeing recruitment posters in 1918, when compulsory recruitment had been introduced in the early months of 1916 is certainly curious. The credibility of Abbott's recollection is questionable.

Max Arthur's *Forgotten Voices of The Great War*, published in association with the Imperial War Museum in 2006, featured two fascinating witnesses who recorded their experiences of seeing posters featuring Kitchener, although only one seems credible. Private Thomas McIndoe of the 12th Battalion, Middlesex Regiment, recounted the reason why he enlisted: 'It was seeing the picture of Kitchener and his finger pointing at you – any position that you took up the finger was always pointing at you – it was a wonderful poster really.' McIndoe probably saw the poster(s) in north London. Whereas Marjorie Llewellyn recalled: 'As a young schoolgirl

I remember there was great excitement in Sheffield when the posters went up showing Kitchener saying "We Want You" and a number of our young men joined up – they were the pick of the city.' Her recollection is at odds with recorded posters, as no known examples featuring Leete's war cartoon bears the slogan 'We Want You'.

Posters, posters everywhere

Examinations of photographic material from various private collections and public archives, including those of the Imperial War Museum, reveal some significant sightings of recruitment posters designed for Britain and the British Empire. They were displayed in likely places such as public hoardings, as well as in and around recruitment centres, railway stations and the London Underground (which, with the support of Frank Pick, commissioned work by Frank Brangywn and

Gerald Spencer Pryse – some of these posters were sent to the Front), also in town squares and city centres, within commercial and public buildings, on taxi-cabs, as well as the exteriors of buses and trams, which traditionally carried advertising.

Within these black and white photographs you can pick out images of beckoning and pointing fingers, as well as some outstretched and waving arms, however, these images are notable for not being the work of Leete. To date, no photographs taken in Britain have yet been traced that show the public posting of the BRITONS – Wants YOU poster, or the David Allen and Sons variant.

A series of photographs taken inside a Montreal recruiting station, circa 1916–17, provides clear evidence of what was actually on display, including many recruitment posters from Britain. Only one poster of Canadian origin can be seen that was inspired by Leete's cartoon design. It was produced in 1915 for Montreal, and featured the words 'Let his heart a thousandfold Take the field again! Are YOU One Of KITCHENER'S OWN?' The BRITONS – Wants YOU poster is conspicuous by its absence (see illustration on page 99).

An extensive article, entitled 'Recruiting By Poster – A remarkable Patriotic Campaign', published by the *Windsor Magazine* (No. 246, June 1915), featured nineteen illustrated examples, although there was no reference to Leete's Kitchener poster – all those profiled being PRC designs.

The keenest observational descriptions of British recruitment posters can be found in the publication *Through French Eyes – Britain's Effort*, written by Henry David Davray and published before the end of the war by Constable and Company in 1916. Some of his recollections are reminiscent of Leete's *London Opinion* poster and the David Allen and Sons variant, although they were in fact different designs.

Davray (1873–1944) was a Frenchman and an Anglophile who worked as a writer and translator in London during the war. At the height of the recruitment period he observed: 'Any Englishman of more than 18 and less than 40 years of age who has failed to enlist must feel remarkably uneasy in his conscience. Which-ever way he looks, bills, placards, posters din into this brain the implacable injunction: "Your Country Needs YOU! Enlist immediately!" It is useless for him to turn away his head, for in that case, not only is he elbowed by ten of his compatriots in khaki, but suddenly his ears are greeted with the warlike strains of the military band preceding a detachment on its way to some railway station or barracks.'

He continued: 'Everything reminds him [the Englishman] that the Empire is at war. On the walls, on the monuments, on the fronts of taxis, in the shop-windows, in the restaurants, the trains, the railway stations, on the motor-buses, in the churches and chapels, in the theatres and cinemas, even in the lavatories, there are bills and placards of all sizes to remind him that the British Empire is defending its existence, and that "Kitchener needs more men". It is impossible not to see them and read them.'

Davray noted that one poster of Kitchener was especially popular, depicting 'on the left, the stern and enigmatic countenance of Lord Kitchener, whilst on the right, are printed a few sentences from the famous speech which the Minister for War delivered at the Guildhall

[9th July 1915].' However, this poster was not a Leete design but rather the PRC poster with Kitchener's words 'Men, Materials & Money Are The Immediate Necessities. Does The Call Of Duty Find No Response In You Until Reinforced – Let Us Rather Say Superseded – By The Call Of Compulsion?' This was officially known as the LORD KITCHENER poster and printed in two versions of different sizes: PRC 113 (20 x 30 inches) and PRC 117 (40 x 50 inches). The poster featured a close-up image of Kitchener's face and part of his shoulders, referred to by Davray as 'the stern and enigmatic countenance…' There was no outstretched arm or pointing finger. By comparison with Leete's striking cartoon, this PRC creation was a dull design.

A Stereoview card produced by the Realistic Travels company depicted Kitchener on a balcony at the Guildhall with the Lord Mayor of London. The card was captioned 'The call which resounded around the world; Lord Kitchener's magic appeal for men' and depicted three pictorial posters affixed to the walls of the building: HE'S HAPPY & SATISFIED – ARE YOU? (PRC 96, printed by Turner and Dunnett); BE READY! (PRC 81, printed by David Allen and Sons); and AN APPEAL TO YOU (PRC 88, printed by Roberts and Leete). This final poster included a soldier with a beckoning finger, which some viewers may well have mistaken for Leete's arm-stretching, finger-pointing design. This image was also used for an Australian poster.

The official 'Lord Kitchener' poster.

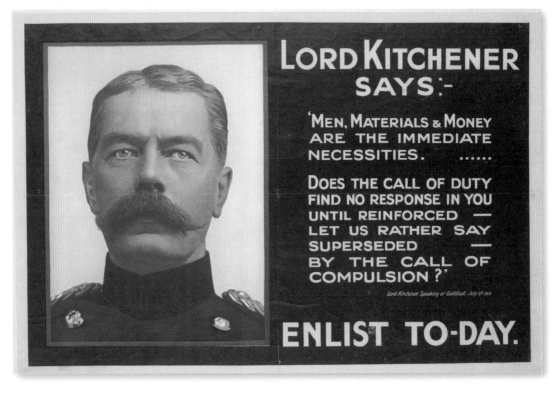

Stereoview of Lord Kitchener at the Guildhall, London.

Lord Kitchener: A *Boy's Own* hero

Henry Davray was an ardent admirer of Kitchener and he relished the times that he was able to observe him in public: 'I have seen Lord Kitchener in civilian attire; I have seen him in the sombre blue uniform of a field-marshal; I saw him at the Guildhall when he delivered, or rather read, a speech on recruiting. In each case, he was a fine figure, though perhaps a little stern and unbending. "I am a soldier," he repeats, when he has to appear at these assemblies; and perhaps he is apologising for an embarrassment which is not discernible, but which he must feel, in spite of the cheers and acclamations which greet him. But it was in his khaki costume that Lord Kitchener really gave me the impression of a leader. Buttoned up in a dark-coloured jacket or tunic, he is the officer in mufti, whom we can recognise among a thousand; but he is a "soldier" from head to foot in his field uniform, with his spurs, his leather gaiters, his ample riding-breeches, his loosely-fitting tunic held in at the waist by a belt of yellow leather supported by a shoulder-piece. The red and gold decoration on the collar, the red band on the cap, and, on the peak, the double garland of gold leaves, are the distinctive signs of rank.'

He went on to describe Kitchener's physical appearance: 'In London, in public, the face is, so to speak, closed, the features are immobile; the solid jaw and the heavy moustache (still very fair) give an impression of strong will, the sternness of which is belied by the blue eyes, which express a kind of astonishment, doubtless the result of a strong desire to be somewhere else. As I saw him, during the whole of that day, the eyelids lowered over the eyes robbed them of that look of astonishment and rendered them, on the contrary, keen and penetrating. With untiring persistence he surveyed and inspected the soldiers, rank after rank.'

In another of Davray's publications of 1916, entitled *Lord Kitchener, His Work and Prestige* (T. Fisher Unwin, London), he extolled the virtues of the British Secretary of State for War.

The introduction, written by Paul Cambon, the Ambassador of the French Republic in London, also highlighted the support Kitchener had given to France during the war.

He wrote: 'I have been for a long time in touch with that great servant of his country, but after the beginning of the war we were brought closer together, and had frequently to meet to discuss the manifold questions which were continually confronting our Governments… This grave, silent, rarely smiling man, who seemed a stranger to all emotion, displayed in personal contact qualities of the heart and a sensibility of which no one, at first, would have thought him capable. Reserved and secret as he was with men whose character he had not tested, he was open and confiding with those whose honesty and discretion he had been able to appreciate…

'[H]e had the art of making men obey him. He knew that authority can be won only by commanding respect, and that excessive familiarity, empty words, and an effusive manner detract from the power to command… A strong will, a clear head, and also, it should be said, an uncommon aptness in judgment, gave him the authority and the prestige which he used at the outbreak of war in making that appeal to England to which the country responded with so huge an impulse.'

Both Cambon and Davray agreed that 'Lord Kitchener was one of the most faithful friends of France'. These publications may well contain genuine sentiments but they can also be read as British propaganda. Prior to World War I, some anti-British propaganda was published in the French satirical magazine *L'Assiette au Buerre*. One notable example created by the artist and cartoonist Jean Veber depicted Lord Kitchener as a toad astride a mass of

Herkomer's portrait of Kitchener.

dead, bloodied bodies – a reference to the brutal behaviour of the British in South Africa during the Boer War, when camps were used to imprison civilians (that gave rise later to the term 'concentration camp').

Field Marshal Horatio Herbert Kitchener, 1st Earl Kitchener KG, KP, GCB, OM, GCSI, GCMG, GCIE, ADC, PC (1850–1916), was a highly decorated soldier, whose first name brings to mind the heroic deeds and derring-do of Vice-Admiral Lord Horatio Nelson (1758–1805). Not surprisingly, images of Nelson were also used for World War I recruitment posters. Aping Nelson, Kitchener also became a *Boy's Own* hero, and, for many, an immensely popular one. One notable portrait of Kitchener in oils, dating from 1890, hangs on public display in the National Portrait Gallery, London, alongside that of Robert Baden-Powell, 1st Baron Baden-Powell. Both paintings are the work of the well-known society portraitist and art teacher Hubert von Herkomer (although the background of Kitchener's portrait was painted by landscape painter Frederick Goodall RA, celebrated for his Egyptian views). Baden-Powell was also noted for his military achievements and hailed as 'The Hero of Mafeking'. Today he is best known as the founding father of the Scout movement, but he also made a personal contribution to the World War I recruitment campaign by designing what became a highly regarded poster of 1915, entitled ARE YOU IN THIS? (PRC 112).

Kitchener was an Irish-born British field marshal and proconsul who won fame for his imperial campaigns. Born at Ballylongford in County Kerry, he was the son of a British army colonel, Henry Horatio Kitchener. His mother, Ann, had died of tuberculosis in 1864. The family had moved to Switzerland in the hope of improving her medical condition but to no avail. Kitchener was tutored privately, received some schooling in Switzerland and after returning to England he also studied and trained at the Royal Military Academy, Woolwich, and later at the School of Military Engineering at Chatham in Kent.[8]

Between 1871 and 1914, Kitchener had a varied but highly successful career. He worked for the Palestine Expedition Fund (PEF) on a mapping survey of the Holy Land that produced lasting results, and later served as a Vice-Consul in Anatolia. From 1884 to 1885, he served as a captain during the Nile Campaign. His human frailties became evident when he suffered a jaw wound during a skirmish, and he recuperated in England before returning to active service.

In 1889, Kitchener took part in the Battle of Toski, which brought an end to the threat of the Mahdist Sudanese in Egypt. When in command of his men, he ensured that his officers could speak Arabic, as he himself could do, to enable more effective communication and arguably better relations with the local people. At this time, before allegations of brutality appeared in relation to his military triumphs in the late 1890s, there were reports of Kitchener's fairness and good standing among his officers, men and subordinates.

But what really brought Kitchener into the public spotlight to ensure him widespread and longstanding popular acclaim was the campaign that started in 1896 when, as Major General, he led British and Egyptian forces up the Nile.

Baden-Powell's recruitment poster.

Are YOU in this?

He did his duty.
Will YOU do YOURS?

War hero Field Marshal Frederick Roberts.

Field Marshal Frederick Roberts, 1st Earl Roberts (1832–1914), was one of the most successful British commanders of the nineteenth century. In 1858, he had been awarded the Victoria Cross (VC) the highest military decoration awarded for valour 'in the face of the enemy', an accolade that eluded Kitchener. In 1915, after his death, Roberts' portrait also featured in a successful PRC recruitment poster, HE DID HIS DUTY. WILL YOU DO YOURS?, of which 95,000 copies were printed. Emulating Roberts' career path, from 1902 to 1909, Kitchener was appointed Commander-in-Chief of the Army of India, later returning to Egypt as British Agent and Consul-General.

Although Kitchener enjoyed phenomenal popularity during his lifetime and after his death, with his portrait painted and sculpted by fine artists, and his features adorning a wide range of wartime memorabilia that included matchboxes and matchcovers, tins and toys (including a Kitchener doll), he did have his detractors. Military historian Peter Simkins revealed some of the negative aspects of his character: 'Although his impressive list of achievements had made him a national hero, Kitchener had a number of serious weaknesses which grew more pronounced at his career prospered. His intolerance of interference and opposition, his seemingly boundless capacity for hard work and his constitutional inability to delegate responsibility all encouraged him to disregard normal

He helped to construct a railway to ensure the supply of arms and reinforcements, and played a significant role in defeating the Sudanese at the Battle of Omdurman, near Khartoum, on 2nd September 1898, thus helping to secure control of the Sudan in north-east Africa, after which he was given the title 'Lord Kitchener of Khartoum'. As Chief of Staff (1900–02) in the Second Boer War he played a key role in Lord Roberts' conquest of the Boer Republics, and later succeeded Roberts as Commander-in-Chief.[9]

procedures and to act as his own chief of staff and military secretary.'

Winston Churchill wrote: '[Kitchener] treated all men like machines, from the private soldier whose salute he disdained, to the superior officers he rigidly controlled… The stern and unpitying spirit of the Commander was communicated to the troops, and the victories which marked the progress of the River War were accompanied by acts of barbarity not always justified even by the harsh custom of savage conflicts or the fierce and treacherous nature of the Dervish.'[10]

The Italian historian Carlo Ginzburg described Kitchener as 'a harsh, ruthless, implacable soldier, a skilful military organizer; a faithful servant of the British Empire across the continents – from Africa, to Australia, to India'. George Warrington Steevens, the journalist and war correspondent for the *Daily Mail* whose accounts of Kitchener's exploits helped to make him famous, believed Kitchener to be 'The Man Who Has Made Himself a Machine'.

Indeed Kitchener was seen by some as being a distant and stern figure, but at the same time he was also widely admired as a tough man needed for tough times, and many thought he was the right man for the job. In fact, according to some sources, if the story is to be believed, it has been claimed that initially he had no desire to take up the position of Secretary of State for War. He was persuaded, in part, by a public appeal launched in the national newspapers, notably *The Times*, which on 3rd August 1914 published an article urging the Prime Minster, Lord Asquith, to offer the position as Secretary of War to Kitchener, the outgoing governor of Egypt.

The campaigns in *The Times* continued and on 5th August the paper launched a full-scale attack against Kitchener's main rival, Richard Haldane, the Lord Chancellor. The writer of this attack was Eton- and Sandhurst-educated war correspondent Lieutenant Colonel Charles à Court Repington, who had served with Kitchener during the Sudan campaign. On the evening of 5th August, no doubt influenced by popular opinion and pressure from the national press, the Prime Minister offered Kitchener the position. However, Kitchener would ultimately fail to win over the trust of all his Cabinet colleagues.

It is known that later in the war some politicians disliked Kitchener for misjudging the amount and type of ammunition needed by the military. Perhaps, in part, the shortage of shells helps to explain the scathing comment attributed to Lady Asquith, the wife of the Prime Minister Herbert Henry Asquith, 1st Earl of Oxford and Asquith. She claimed he was 'A poor general, but a wonderful poster'. Later, she assigned this quote to her daughter. Kitchener has also been described as 'a good poster and poor administrator'.

Lady Asquith was not the first to describe Kitchener in this manner – as Hiley has observed, that particular honour falls to Sir Arthur Markham, Liberal MP for Mansfield. It was recorded by Hansard (House of Commons Debates, 31 May 1916, volume 82, column 2807) that Sir Arthur Markham made an attack on Kitchener, including the statement: 'Lord Kitchener, we all know, is a great poster, and has been very successful as a poster, but what happened with regard to recruiting?' Both Markham and Lady Asquith were almost certainly referring to the PRC 'Lord Kitchener' poster (as opposed to the Leete design) as this was known through the official PRC records

"CARRY ON!"

By kind permission of 'London Opinion'.

68 T ROTARY PHOTO, £.C.   THE LATE EARL KITCHENER, WAR MINISTER.
"WHO BEING DEAD YET SPEAKETH."

Photo-card of Lord Kitchener 'Who Being Dead Yet Speaketh'.

to have been the most popular recruitment poster of the war.

David Lloyd George, who had replaced Asquith as Prime Minister in December 1916, unfairly endorsed this view. Kitchener accurately predicted, against popular political opinion, that the war would be a long one of at least three years needing millions of men, and when he was in office he started planning immediately to raise the necessary men to fight it. Kitchener's popularity was such that when Alfred Harmsworth, the press baron better known as Lord Northcliffe, a pioneer of tabloid journalism who owned both *The Times* and the *Daily Mail*, dared to criticise him in the pages of the *Mail*, it led to copies being burnt in the London Stock Exchange.

Kitchener's eyes also attracted critical and public attention. Once seen, they left a lasting impression. A contemporary journalist wrote that 'their colour is quite beautiful – as deep and as clear a blue as the sea, in its most azure moments – and they look out at the world, with the perfect directness of a man who sees straight to his end'. Another journalist observed: 'About the eyes of Kitchener it may be said without offence that the terror they inspire is heightened by a squint which has tended to grow more pronounced with age. The eyes are blue, penetrating, and full of judgment; without their irregularity, they would be difficult eyes to face, but with this irregularity they fill certain men with a veritable paralysis of terror.'

Kitchener's own end was a tragic one and it added greatly to the myths that surrounded him. In June 1916, sailing on a diplomatic mission to Russia aboard HMS *Hampshire*, his ship hit a mine and sank west of the Orkney Islands. Kitchener, his staff and almost all the crew perished. His body was never recovered. There was national mourning, and later a memorial was created and placed in All Souls' Chapel at St. Paul's Cathedral.

Several posters and photo-cards were produced after his death – his reputation and image still being deemed of valuable assistance to encourage recruitment and bolster morale. One such photo-card of 1916, held in the private collection of Hiley, featured a fairly accurate photographic recreation of Leete's cover design for *London Opinion* for 5th September 1914. It was created by the Rotary Photo Company and the card carried the slogan and strapline 'Carry On! By kind permission of

"*London Opinion*" – The Late Earl Kitchener, War Minister, "Who Being Dead Yet Speaketh".

The genesis of Leete's design

A close examination of the 'Carry On!' photo-card under magnification reveals that on Kitchener's collar, just below his thumb, there is a name in white: 'Bassano'. Alexander Bassano (1829–1913) was the leading high society portrait photographer of the Victorian era. The National Portrait Gallery (NPG) in London holds a large collection of material from his company dating from the 1870s to the 1940s, of which 2,708 portraits are directly attributable to Alexander Bassano. Between 1876 and 1921, his studio was based at 25, Old Bond Street, London, and it was almost certainly here that he photographed Kitchener. This studio was large enough to accommodate an eighty-foot panoramic background scene mounted on rollers, which provided a variety of outdoor scenes or court backgrounds. Bassano retired from work at the studio in around 1903, although the firm continued and acquired other companies until it closed down in 1974.[11]

Bassano personally photographed many members of the British and European royal families, including Queen Victoria, King Edward VII, Queen Mary and Alfonso XII (King of Spain), along with aristocrats, the rich and the famous, as well as politicians such as William Ewart Gladstone. He produced more than one hundred portraits of Kitchener, ranging from full-lengths in military uniform to informal head-and-shoulder shots. Several of these photographs were created as cabinet cards, a larger version of the earlier *carte de visite* popular in the 1870s.

One such cabinet card of 1885 from the NPG collections features a close-up view of Kitchener's head and part of his shoulders. This type of view was more unusual than the standard shots taken at a distance and has been considered as a possible source for Alfred Leete's portrait head design. In terms of actual image size, this photograph measures only 5⅝ x 4 inches (NPG reference: x127983).

However, there are several other Bassano photographs that are also potential matches, including a cabinet card dated 1895 (NPG reference: x127982) and also a half-plate glass negative dating from 1900 (NPG reference: x96369). The latter is arguably the closest match to Leete's cartoon cover design and was almost certainly the primary source for the PRC's LORD KITCHENER poster produced in 1915. The 'YOU Are The Man I Want' picture postcard also derived from the Bassano half-plate negative x96369, and the photographic image also appeared on Wills cigarette cards. In addition, the Rotary Photo Company produced a postcard of Lord Kitchener during his lifetime, which derived from the same photographic

source. Entitled 'Kitchener's Counsel to Soldiers', it concluded with the words 'Do Your Duty Bravely. Fear God. Honour The King'.

All of these cards, Leete's cartoon and the associated posters, portrayed a much younger looking and fuller-faced Kitchener than was actually the case in the early period of the war. To that end, these images acted as propaganda.

The Imperial War Museum has claimed that one of its photographs of Kitchener (IWM reference: Q56739) is the primary source referenced by Leete. However, although their portrait portrays Kitchener wearing his hat (which Leete could have seen in many other photographs to incorporate into his artwork), the thinner features and wearied expression do not correlate closely to the *London Opinion* cartoon cover or the BRITONS – WANTS YOU poster. The IWM website does not reveal a photographer for the image Q56739, but it does appear in the *Lord Kitchener Memorial Book* credited to the British photographers Elliott and Fry and was described as 'one of the latest portraits of Lord Kitchener' – and therefore dates from late in 1915, or even the early months of 1916.

It is known that Kitchener visited Bassano's studio several times, as there are photographs dating from 1888, 1895, 1900 and the last known in 1910. Many other photographers took his portrait and they included: Otto Schoefft, who produced photographic

cabinet cards of him in the mid-1880s, G. Lekegian and Co. in 1898, as well as Duffus Bros. in 1901. However, their photos are not such close matches to Leete's design.

Leete had copied one or more of Bassano's photographs, and perhaps some others too, in order to produce his design featuring Kitchener. For a cartoonist and commercial illustrator working at that time, this activity was far from unusual, and in a wartime situation many would have regarded it as morally justifiable. This was a period before the widespread

'I Say! U Try' poster, featuring, on the wall behind the boy, a pointing man.

introduction of intellectual property rights and concomitant lawyers. Cartoonists and commercial illustrators were for the most part at liberty to use anything, within the accepted realms of decency. Hiley's photo-card of 1916 bearing the name Bassano was not only cashing in on the death of a popular hero in an acceptable patriotic manner, but acknowledging in a subtle way, perhaps unwittingly, that Leete had borrowed their photograph(s) to create his own design.

Hiley has shown that Leete's novel format of portraying Kitchener with outstretched arm and pointing finger actually derived from two significant commercial sources (although, of course, there is a substantial 'back catalogue' of art-historical images that depict prominent figures with outstretched arms and pointing fingers – Michelangelo's *Creation of Adam* from the Sistine Chapel ceiling in Rome, painted between 1508 and 1512, immediately springs to mind, and is without question a familiar image around the world).

One of the commercial sources can be traced to an advertisement in poster form featured in Howard Bridgewater's *Advertising or the Art of Making Known A Simple Exposition of The Principles of Advertising*, published by Sir Isaac Pitman & Sons, London, in 1910. However, rather than recruiting soldiers, the man in the photograph, James Motherwell, was promoting the sale of Godfrey Phillips & Sons B.D.V. Pure Virginia Cigarettes.[12]

In W.E.D. Allen's history of the family firm of printers, there was a revealing reference to Motherwell: '[A] fine, good-looking man from Belfast who had a long and faithful service with the firm. His face became famous on a nationwide scale. Allens, who did much commercial as well as theatrical work, produced a poster for a famous firm of cigarettes – "B.D.V." It showed a packet of cigarettes and a very good-looking dark man whose eyes were dead centre of the poster and which consequently followed the observer everywhere as did his pointing finger. That man was James Motherwell.'

The second commercial source identified by Hiley, and one that David Allen and Sons may well have drawn upon for their tobacco campaign, is featured on a lantern slide of 1903. The slide depicts a boy in, or near, Southampton, standing beside a wall predominantly pasted with various letterpress posters. One pictorial poster stands out as it depicts a man with captivating gaze and accusing finger with the slogan 'I Say! U Try', promoting the company name Antelope Furnishing Stores. From such visual evidence it is clear that this promotional format was already familiar in parts of Britain through the medium of commercial advertising at least ten years before the start of World War I.

Further sources for the novel format include various Victorian and Edwardian advertisements and theatrical poster designs that use images of hands with pointing fingers, albeit usually detached from a human body.

A striking image and concise slogan

The whereabouts of the records indicating exactly how many of Leete's posters were printed and precisely where they were distributed have not been located, if indeed they were ever collated. In 1954, *London Opinion* was acquired by *Men Only* magazine, known for its robust adult humour, and because of dwindling sales in April of that year, it was promptly shut down. It is likely that the print run for the *London Opinion* BRITONS – WANTS YOU poster was in the low thousands – around 5,000, or less – and a comparable figure is also likely for the David Allen and Sons version.[13]

Only four PRC posters exceeded 100,000. In ascending order of popularity they were: WE'RE BOTH NEEDED TO SERVE THE GUNS! FILL UP THE RANKS! PILE UP THE MUNITIONS! (101,000); TAKE UP THE SWORD OF JUSTICE (105,000); REMEMBER BELGIUM (140,000) and LORD KITCHENER (145,000).[14] As discussed earlier, this final poster was not Leete's design, but the official poster that did not feature the famous pointing finger.

If posters featuring Leete's Kitchener design issued by *London Opinion*, or for that matter the David Allen and Sons variant, were really so popular and attracted the widespread

attention that some writers have claimed, then surely far more copies would have survived today and be found in private and public collections? Britain's national collection of posters is held by the Victoria and Albert Museum, but it does not hold any copies of Leete's Kitchener designs in poster form. In fact, at the time of writing, the only public collection in England that holds authentic examples is the Imperial War Museum: one *London Opinion* poster and one of the David Allen and Sons variant.

The scarcity of Leete's recruitment posters is also borne out by auction house records. Patrick Bogue, the director of Onslow Auctions, which specialises in posters, has described the BRITONS – WANTS YOU poster as 'very rare… we have never sold it', and 'the David Allen version is rare too'. The Poster

More than 100,000 copies of this PRC poster were printed.

Department of Christie's, South Kensington, could trace no historic or current sales records of Leete's Kitchener design.

A recent examination of Imperial War Museum records by Richard Slocombe, the IWM's Senior Curator of Art, has shown that the BRITONS – Wants YOU poster was not donated to the museum by Leete, but was almost certainly the one discovered in March 1951 by Lt-Col. F. Hervey in the cellars of the London Central Recruiting Depot in Great Scotland Yard. For some inexplicable reason the IWM records are not accurate for this period and so it is not possible to reveal a precise date for when the poster was formally acquired for the collections, however, it is likely to have been in the 1950s. The story of the poster's discovery featured in the *News Chronicle*. Slocombe recounted: 'Bradley [the former curator who by this time was Director-General of the IWM] was desperate to see the poster after the story broke. His desperation to see the poster suggests that we did not have our copy by this time, otherwise why the great urgency to see it?'

Robert Opie, the consumer historian and man behind the private Museum of Brands, Packaging and Advertising in Notting Hill, London, believes he owns a BRITONS – Wants YOU poster. It has featured on the contents page (almost full-page) in his lavishly illustrated compilation, *1910s Scrapbook: The Decade of the Great War* (Pi Global Publishing, 2000). By reproducing his poster on such a large scale (the publication measures around 36 x 25 cm), the prominence of this recruitment poster has been overstated in relation to the other examples featured, notably the PRC's Lord Kitchener design, which is also illustrated although at a considerably smaller size. His poster is not on

display and requests to examine the item to check its authenticity were turned down on the grounds that it was too fragile to be moved. However, examination of the detailed photographs point positively towards the opinion that this is indeed an authentic poster.

The Australian War Memorial (AWM) also claims to hold a rare example of Alfred Leete's BRITONS – Wants YOU poster (AWM reference: ARTV04085, date made: c.1914–1916). However, when the author examined it in August 2012, it turned out to be a later reproduction. It is inscribed with the details of a second printer and also a publisher – 'The Curwen Press, Ltd. [Printer], Her Majesty's Stationery Office [Publisher]' – along with the numeric details '*Dmd. 386043/10/68*'. The poster was almost certainly printed in 1968 for sale in various retail outlets to benefit the IWM. The price paid by the AWM for its 'rare period poster' was not revealed.

Kitchener was posted across Great Britain and parts of the British Empire, but the posters were predominantly the PRC Lord Kitchener designs. By modern standards, the design of this and other PRC posters is weak in comparison to Leete's design, and the slogans are often limp, too. Many of the PRC posters were created by committees. It was the subject of Kitchener himself, rather than the design of this official poster and others, that made them immensely popular.

Interestingly, neither the Lord Kitchener posters nor Leete's war cartoon featured in the set of twelve cigarette cards collectively called 'Recruitment Posters', produced by W.D. & H.O. Wills in 1915, or the Wills set published for Australia. On the back of each card of the British set, it stated that each poster was published by the Parliamentary Recruiting Committee,

except for RALLY ROUND THE FLAG. The tobacco company selected many of the popular posters that included (in alphabetical order): 'ANOTHER CALL'; COME ALONG, BOYS!; "FALL IN"; FOLLOW ME!; HE DID HIS DUTY. WILL YOU DO YOURS?; LINE UP, BOYS!; RALLY ROUND THE FLAG; REMEMBER BELGIUM; THE "SCRAP OF PAPER"; THERE IS STILL A PLACE IN THE LINE FOR YOU; THINK!; and WHAT IN THE END WILL SETTLE THIS WAR?[15]

If the *London Opinion* poster of Kitchener had captivated public attention during the war years, it would be reasonable to expect far more contemporary critical notice. Leete was certainly conscious of the success of his cartoon and decided to create variants and parodies himself in following issues of *London Opinion*. On the cover of the 14th November 1914 issue, he created a cartoon captioned 'Wanted', which depicted an imagined YOUR COUNTRY NEEDS YOU poster affixed to a wall with the outstretched arm of Kitchener, his sleeve bearing the word 'Conscription', about to grab an unsuspecting city gentleman.

In the same issue, Leete had another smaller cartoon featured, which portrayed a carpenter holding a plank of wood and bag of tools talking to an old bearded man beside a wall displaying the official recruiting poster, YOUR KING & COUNTRY NEEDS YOU. The captions reveal the dry sense of humour and love of double meaning that made Leete such a popular cartoonist – The Old 'Un: 'How is it you ain't gone for a soldier?' The Young 'Un: 'Ow could I? I'm on piece work.'

There is one notable independent parody of Leete's design, captioned 'Why Are YOU Still in Khaki?', and published in black and white in *The Bystander* on 25th August 1915. Created by Dundee-born commercial artist and poster designer Alick Ritchie (1868–1938), it was one of three images forming his main design, accompanied by the slogan 'Some Recruiting From The Army Posters – Hints for the Peace Office when the time comes for recruiting for Civilian Ranks'.[16]

In addition, there is one colour postcard design in Hiley's private collection by Sidney

Atkinson Potts (1886–1962). It is from circa 1914 and features the words 'It's YOU I Want! – Please Sir! I Didn't Break It!!' Potts was a press artist living and working in London during the war years. As such he would have been familiar with the latest covers and images of the London magazines. He may have viewed a poster featuring Leete's Kitchener cartoon, but he was more likely to have seen the cover of *London Opinion* of 5th September 1914. It is the only known contemporary comic send-up in colour inspired by Leete's Kitchener cartoon.

Leete's original artwork of Lord Kitchener for *London Opinion* was excluded from the exhibition of war posters put on tour by the Imperial War Museum in 1917, however, it was included in the prestigious exhibition of war posters in 1919 at the Grafton Galleries, London. As several propaganda poster specialists have observed, including Jim Aulich, the contributor of Alfred Leete's entry in the *Oxford Dictionary of National Biography*, 'the inclusion of this artwork design in that exhibition is the likely explanation for why it has so often been mistakenly reproduced as a published poster'.

After entering the IWM collections, it was catalogued as part of the poster collections and this also explains the confusion that still surrounds its original creation and purpose.

Certainly Leete's forceful Lord Kitchener cartoon attracted various printers and publishers to the potential of adapting it for posters in Britain and abroad. But the remarkable familiarity with Leete's cartoon issued as a poster by *London Opinion* derives only from a much later post-war period following its acquisition by the IWM in the 1950s, and when it became widely available to see in reproductions and in digital form in fairly recent decades.

Leete's war cartoon 'Your Country Needs YOU' is striking and the slogan easy to recall compared to the longer caption of the *London Opinion* poster, BRITONS – WANTS YOU – JOIN YOUR COUNTRY'S ARMY! GOD SAVE THE KING. It should also be borne in mind that the slogan 'Your Country Needs YOU' has universal appeal as clearly it could apply to any country, whereas the caption of the *London Opinion* poster has limited appeal to those only with a kinship or sympathy to Britain. For many people, Leete's 'Your Country Needs YOU' cartoon has become the dominant recruitment image of World War I simply because the slogan is the only one that readily springs to mind.

Across: Four of the twelve 'Recruitment Posters' cigarette cards.
Below: Spoof of the Kitchener cartoon.

PLEASE SIR! I DIDN'T BREAK IT !!

WHO'S ABSENT?

Is it You?

PUBLISHED BY THE PARLIAMENTARY RECRUITING COMMITTEE, LONDON. POSTER NO. 125   PRINTED BY ANDREW REID & CO., LTD., 50, GREY STREET, NEWCASTLE-ON-TYNE.

CHAPTER 2

WEAPONS OF MASS PERSUASION

ORIGINS, DEVELOPMENT AND DESIGN OF BRITISH RECRUITMENT POSTERS IN WORLD WAR I

On 28th June 1914, the assassination of Archduke Franz Ferdinand of Austria destabilised the delicate allegiances and power-pacts of world politics. It sparked off a war that was driven to a large extent by the vexatious nature, imperial ambitions and warmongering of Wilhelm II, the German Emperor and King of Prussia. It was a war that would change the lives of millions of people around the world. More than fifty million (some sources suggest sixty and even seventy) military personnel were mobilised and over nine million combatants were killed. Entire generations of young men from towns and villages across Europe were wiped out. The conflict drew in the global powers. The Entente powers and their allies were pitched against the Central powers. The former comprised Australia and New Zealand, Brazil, Canada, China, France, Greece, India, Italy, Japan, Montenegro, Newfoundland, Portugal, Romania, Russia, Serbia and South Africa and the United States of America among others; and the latter Austria-Hungary, Bulgaria, Germany and the Ottoman Empire.[17]

Britain was not the only country taken by surprise at the audacious actions of Germany, which had signed the 1839 Treaty of London guaranteeing the neutrality of Belgium. This treaty was effectively ripped up when Kaiser Wilhelm approved the invasion of that country on 2nd August 1914. Luxembourg was taken quickly and by 20th August, the German army had entered Brussels. Allied propaganda commenced immediately, stating categorically that as Germany had not respected this international treaty then the country was not to be trusted.

A PRC propaganda poster entitled The "Scrap of Paper" featured a photographic copy of the original 1839 agreement with the signatories of the six plenipotentiaries to the treaty, contemptuously referred to by the German Chancellor as 'a scrap of paper'. Printed in December 1914, it was displayed throughout Britain and exported to sympathetic countries abroad. Also in December 1914, the PRC created what became an immensely popular poster: Remember Belgium. Produced in two different sizes, the PRC records indicate that this was the second most popular poster in terms of numbers.[18]

In defence of Belgium, and fearful of invasion threats, Britain declared war on Germany on 4th August 1914. Britain's 'Senior Service', the Royal Navy, boasted some of the most technically advanced battleships, known as 'dreadnoughts' after HMS *Dreadnought*. In 1906, when this revolutionary ship entered active

Across: Poster showing the 1839 agreement, or 'scrap of paper'.

Below: Leeds Pals (see page 75).

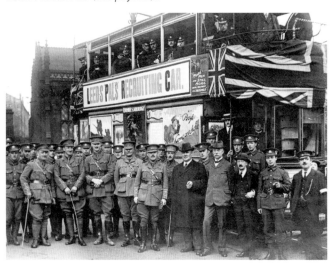

THE "SCRAP OF PAPER"

These are the signatures and seals of the representatives
of the Six Powers to the "Scrap of Paper"——the Treaty
signed in 1839 guaranteeing the independence and
neutrality of Belgium.
"Palmerston" signed for Britain. "Bülow" for Prussia.

The Germans have broken their pledged word
and devastated Belgium. Help to keep your
Country's honour bright by restoring Belgium
her liberty.

ENLIST TO-DAY

JOHNSON, RIDDLE & CO., LTD., LONDON, S.C.   PUBLISHED BY THE PARLIAMENTARY RECRUITING COMMITTEE, LONDON.—POSTER NO. 18—W 4500–5000–6/15

Above and across: Official posters targeted men of various ages and professions.

service, she was fitted with steam turbines, making her the fastest naval ship in the world. Britain had other capital ships, including the *Queen Elizabeth*-class battleships, comprising of five super-dreadnoughts commissioned between 1915 and 1916, which were the first ships to be fitted with 15-inch guns. HMS *Queen Elizabeth* took part in the Dardanelles campaigns of 1915 and four of the ships fought at the Battle of Jutland, 31st May – 1st June 1916.[19]

After the introduction of the 'dreadnoughts', it was not surprising that many other countries wanted to own them or construct comparable vessels. Initially there were serious threats from German U-boats but these lessened in 1917 when convoys were introduced and the war at sea turned into a military stalemate.

In terms of warfare at sea, the Royal Navy enjoyed technological advancements that were in marked contrast to the often inferior and sometimes sub-standard land-based equipment utilised by British military men. For example the English 'Mark I', the world's first combat tank, introduced in 1916, had only varying degrees of success, with many of them developing technical faults and breaking down.

In the air, there were British concerns about Zeppelins. Blimps and Sopwith 'Camels' and 'Snipes' took to the skies and aircraft carriers were utilised for the first time. As the war progressed, aircraft were used as long-range bombers, however, respective air forces were still in their infancy, with the Royal Air Force (RAF) only being formed on 1st April 1918.

Despite all of the technological advances that took place during World War I, the conflict's final outcome would ultimately be determined on land. At the outbreak of war, Britain still possessed a significant naval force maintained by sufficient numbers of sailors. However, it was evident that soldiers were in very short supply.

The 'Call to Arms'

Britain's long history of voluntary recruitment and a Liberal government that was against conscription ensured that – for the first year, at least – men were persuaded to sign up on a voluntary basis. It was also believed that the immediate introduction of conscription would alienate citizens rather than rally them to the defence of their country. The numbers required for the war, that ran longer than was widely predicted, dramatically increased and finally conscription was introduced in stages from January 1916 onwards. Married men were exempt until June of that year, although as Dr Adrian Gregory, lecturer in Modern History at the University of Oxford, has pointed out, those who had 'attested' under the Derby scheme (those married men who had agreed to serve on the understanding that they would be the last to be called up) were enlisted earlier.

Initially the 'Call to Arms' relied upon patriotism and there was no shortage of men coming forward in the early months of war. Patriotism, pride, honour and duty were further awakened through various government and privately sponsored activities, events and schemes that included: comedy, displays, exhibitions, films, lantern slide shows, lectures, marching bands, musical and music hall performances, practical demonstrations, rallies, rousing speeches, singing and the theatre. The British Parliament, pulpit and the pub all played their part in stimulating enthusiasm for war and maintaining an interest in it.[20]

War poetry would also play a part in recruitment, albeit to a limited extent. One of the most memorable poems, 'In Flanders Fields', was created by the Canadian physician Lieutenant-Corporal John Macrae. He was inspired to write it by the loss of a close friend at the Second Battle of Ypres (22nd April – 25th May 1915) in which Germany used poison gas for the first time on a large scale. The poem was later published by *Punch* magazine in London on 8th December 1915. As a result of the poem's popularity, parts of it were used for recruitment purposes. The references to red poppies by the graves of dead servicemen – 'In Flanders fields the poppies blow, Between the crosses, row on row' – helped

to contribute to what has become the world's most memorable memorial symbol.

Recently though, historians of World War I, notably among them the University of Exeter's Dr Catriona Pennell in *A Kingdom United: Popular Responses to the Outbreak of the First World War In Britain and Ireland* (Oxford University Press, 2012), have challenged the popularly-held assumption that most men, and some boys, were largely cheery and happy folk who rushed forward with wide-eyed innocence to take the colours. Pennell argued that the intial rush to enlist was largely driven by a 'dutiful acceptance of the task ahead' in large parts of Britain. In Simkins' groundbreaking *Kitchener's Army*, the crucial point is also made that many joined up as they had been

told by so-called reliable sources that the war would only last a few months. Of course, there were specific groups, such as in Ireland, who were certainly not enamored with the idea of supporting Great Britain, and so specific Irish recruitment campaigns devised by Irish people were implemented to encourage enlistment.

The power of advertising

Adventure, camaraderie, exotic travel, salaries that were better than some occupations at home, as well as free smart uniforms (that were claimed to be alluring to the ladies), were all promoted in posters to encourage enlistment. Some designs were specially designed to spread feelings of guilt and fear. They included German atrocities such as the execution of the British nurse Edith Cavell in Belgium on 12th October 1915, although images of dead servicemen and women were rare in British posters and were usually actively discouraged by the PRC.

Women at home were specifically targeted to back their men and as the war went on they took on new roles and jobs. Some women joined the 'Order of the White Feather' established by Admiral Charles Fitzgerald in August 1914 with support from the prominent author Mrs Humphrey Ward. This organisation encouraged women to hand out a white feather, indicating cowardice, to any man not in uniform. However, it was difficult to differentiate between a shirker and a genuine case of non-enlistment.

Advertising would prove to be a far more effective recruitment method than white feathers. This medium and its methods were not without critics, with discontented voices coming from the British ruling classes who felt that advertising would destabilise the prevailing class system. With varying degrees of enthusiasm and reluctance, the British government enlisted the voluntary services of specialists and consultants from the world of advertising, and the press barons were encouraged to promote the war positively through their newspapers.

Across: Unique posters designed for Ireland. Below: The promise of free uniforms was an incentive to join up.

Hedley Le Bas was one of the leading lights of the advertising industry who recounted how prior to the war he had an important and mutually beneficial meeting on Walton Heath golf course with Sir George Riddell, a fellow director of Caxton Publishing, and the politician and soldier John Edward Bernard Seely, 1st Baron Mottistone, who was, prior to Kitchener, Secretary of State for War. According to Le Bas, Colonel Seely (as he was then ranked) 'happened to turn to me… "Now, you are an old soldier," he said. "Supposing you had to find 35,000 men for the Army, how would you set to work?" My business experience had made me a man with one fixed idea – that publicity will find or create anything. Instantly I answered

Across: Leete's poster for the Tank Corps.
Below: Some posters instilled feelings of guilt.

according to my faith: "I should advertise for them." Colonel Seely, to my surprise, took my answer seriously.'[21]

Le Bas' company was awarded a government contract and £6,000 to generate effective advertising to raise recruits. His campaign commenced on 15th January 1914 and over time this resulted not only in effective newspaper advertising, but also a film promoting the British army.

There was also a new wave of letterpress and pictorial posters, which included the following: THE WAR – FOUR QUESTIONS TO EMPLOYERS (21st December 1914); 5 QUESTIONS TO MEN WHO HAVE NOT ENLISTED (4th January 1915); 4 QUESTIONS TO THE WOMEN OF ENGLAND (13th January 1915); and 5 QUESTIONS TO THOSE WHO EMPLOY MALE SERVANTS (19th January 1915), among many others. Some targeted motor drivers, packers, porters, labourers and navvies, as well as ex-Non-Commissioned officers, clerks, shop assistants and shopkeepers. Posters were specially designed to raise recruits in Ireland and also translated into the Welsh language.[22]

At the outbreak of war in August 1914, there were only 450,000 men in the British army, with 268,000 part-time soldiers in the Territorial Force. Lord Kitchener, the Secretary of State for War, had the foresight to predict that the war would be long and costly. He took immediate steps, with the assistance of Le Bas and others, to expand the army into so-called 'new armies', which were also known collectively as 'Kitchener's Army'. After training, the men of these 'new battalions', some of which were initially privately funded, would join long-standing regiments. Britain's army during the war numbered over five million men, by far the biggest in the nation's history. Remarkably, almost

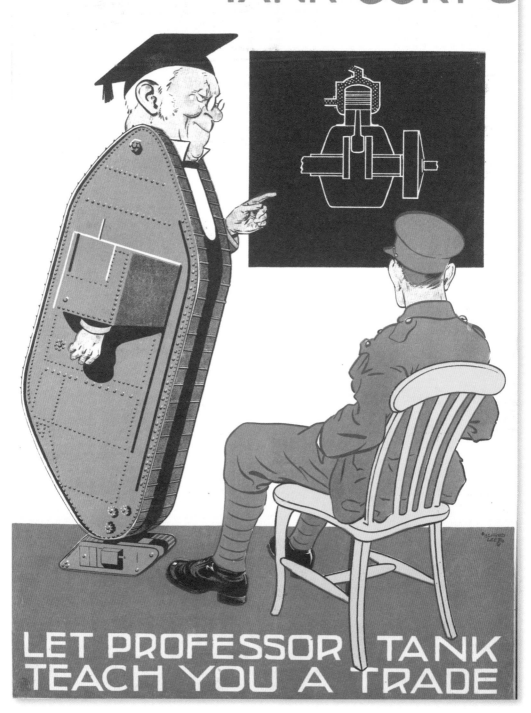

half of those men who served in it were volunteers – an astonishing 2,466,719 men enlisted between August 1914 and December 1915, many in response to the appeals of the Secretary of State of War, Field Marshal Kitchener.

Hedley Le Bas had his work cut out trying to convince Kitchener of the merits of new forms of advertising and poster production. Le Bas was well aware of the popular appeal of Kitchener, recognising that far more people identified positively with this military hero than the king of England. On 6th August 1914, Le Bas approached Kitchener to seek his permission to be featured in a new campaign.

After Kitchener's untimely death, Le Bas lamented the loss of a friend and Britain's most valuable promotional aid. Le Bas edited *The Lord Kitchener Memorial Book*, which was profusely illustrated to mark his life and achievements, although the *London Opinion* poster featuring Leete's Lord Kitchener cartoon was not included. The book was published in 1917 on behalf of the Lord Kitchener National Memorial Fund (of which Le Bas was the honorary organiser) to raise money for injured and disabled servicemen. In it, Le Bas wrote a short chapter, entitled *Advertising For An Army*, in which he outlined the positives of Kitchener's reputation.

Cardiff recruiting station, plastered with posters.

Le Bas 'knew the solid advantages of that wonderful name and personality, with their power to move people and inspire them to patriotic effort. The right to use the name made the enormous task of finding a new army all the easier.'

Le Bas' laudatory comments about Kitchener were admirable in the wake of his death, however, the Secretary of State for War was far from being comfortable with being used for publicity material and remained suspicious of the popular appeals. His conservatism made it extremely difficult to develop an effective and sustained campaign. Le Bas went on record as saying that 'Lord Kitchener! His name made the recruiting campaign possible and vindicated the voluntary system.' However, some of the credit for the success of the appeals should also go to Le Bas. For his services during the war, Le Bas was justly knighted in 1916.[23]

As noted at the beginning of this book, the main official organisation tasked to enlist the men for war was the Parliamentary Recruiting Committee (PRC), an all-party body formed at the end of August 1914. The Prime Minister and leaders of the respective political parties were among its key members. Sub-Departments (SDs) were quickly established and that of 'Publications and Publicity' was tasked with the responsibility of producing a wide range of materials. At that time, posters were undoubtedly the most effective means of mass communication. The first radio station in Britain was only introduced in 1922, and the public at large either did not buy or a notable number could not read magazines and newspapers.

The Publications Sub-Department supervised the most concerted leaflet and poster recruiting drive Britain had ever seen, although at its first meeting on 3rd September 1914, when there was no shortage of recruits, it initially decided that the production of elaborate pictorial posters was not necessary. However, as the mood of the country changed and recruitment slowed, the PRC looked at alternatives to the simplistic and sober party election leaflets being produced at the time to entice recruits, and before Christmas the true power of the recruitment poster had been unleashed. [24]

Poster designs had been subjected to harsh criticism as 'crude woodcuts, displayed haphazardly by the fly-posting system' in the first half of the nineteenth century, however, W.E.D. Allen observed that 'the early lithographs were also of poor quality.' But gradually the standard improved, largely as a result of inspiration from across the Channel, where Cheret, Grasset, Toulouse-Lautrec and many others had turned great artistic talents to the work of posters. Most authorities on the subject agree that the first English poster of real merit was Fred Walker's engraving of 1871, advertising Wilkie Collins's drama, *The Woman in White*.

Other artists of repute entered the field, among them Professor Herkomer [Hubert von Herkomer], E.A. Abbey, W.P. Frith and H. Stacey Marks, all of the Royal Academy. Sir John Millais caused a public sensation by allowing Mr. Barrett, then Managing Director of Pears Soap, to use his 'Bubbles' as an advertisement, though it is possible to doubt whether the painter was aware of Barrett's intentions when the deal was made. And in 1886, Sir Edward J. Poynter, the President of the Royal Academy himself, painted an advertisement for the Guardian Fire and Life Assurance Company, in which he conveyed the dignity of his office by an overpowering arrangement of symmetrical detail framing an over-dressed

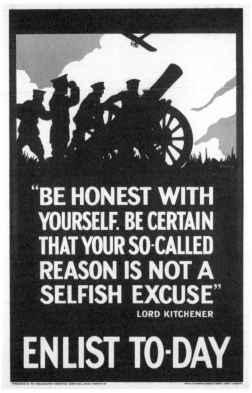

Using Kitchener's name to inspire a patriotic response.

female figure bearing spear, shield and helmet.

Allen continued: 'The ice was clearly broken. But it was not the desultory interest of a few Royal Academicians that blew real life into the poster art. In the closing years of the century there grew up a school of artists, such as Dudley Hardy, the Beggarstaff brothers, Albert Morrow and John Hassall, who put their best work into posters, and did something to support the claim that hoardings were the picture gallery of the poor man.'

In addition there were also considerable advances in technology: 'Display boards were more solidly built, to weather storm and reduce the danger to the public. Billposting companies began to treat their stations as harmonious units, with bills neatly bordered and framed,

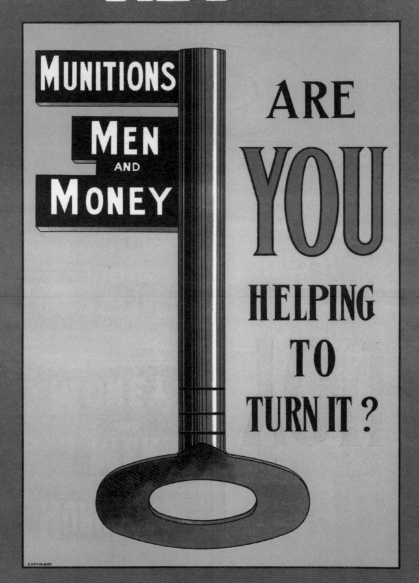

THE **KEY** TO THE

MUNITIONS
MEN AND **MONEY**

ARE
YOU
HELPING
TO
TURN IT ?

COPYRIGHT.

SITUATION

PUBLISHED BY THE PARLIAMENTARY RECRUITING COMMITTEE, LONDON. POSTER Nº 116   PRINTED BY SPARGEANT BROS. LTD. LONDON & ABERGAVENNY.

and displayed with an eye to balance of colour and design. The result of improved craftsmanship was a marked change in public opinion, even affecting the hard core of S.C.A.P.A. itself.' The Society for Checking the Abuses of Public Advertising SCAPA was founded in 1893.

Alas, the PRC committees were notable for being made up of administrators, clerks and managers. They lacked valuable in-house expertise relating to commercial and fine arts or the business of printing and publishing that would have been of practical benefit for the production of posters. So perhaps it is not surprising that early attempts were roundly criticised as the first official designs were largely unimaginative creations. This encouraged Le Bas to form his own Advisory Committee, taking initiative from H.E. Morgan, who was in charge of the publicity departments of W.H. Smith and Son. The government had refused to recognise Morgan's committee but heeded his criticisms. Morgan described the early efforts of poster design in far from glowing terms, claiming them to be 'such gross waste of space, such lack of imagination, such commonplace utterances and phrases given such sheer physical publicity'.

According to Hiley, Le Bas' committee comprised 'Wareham Smith and Thomas Russell, veterans of the first War Office campaign… Charles Frederick Higham, an influential advertising agent and editor of *Higham's Magazine*, Henry Simonis, advertising manager of the *Daily News* and John Camille Akerman, managing director of *Advertisers' Weekly* and soon to be advertising manager of *The Times*'. With Le Bas as Chairman and Eric Field as Secretary, they formed the 'Voluntary Recruiting Publicity Committee'. They pledged

Motivational posters featuring Kitchener's words.

to improve the standard of posters. Letterpress posters still had their place but the focus was now on the production of a wide range of pictorial posters that would, it was hoped, bring forth new recruits in significant numbers.

Minutes and records of the PRC's activities and achievements (now held in the National Archives at Kew) indicate that their meetings were held at St. Stephen's Chambers in Westminster, London, and also at Number 12, Downing Street, the official residence of the Parliamentary Secretary to the Treasury.[25] Two black and white photographs now in the collections of the British Library (BL) show the range of the PRC recruitment posters on the walls of the large Reception Room in Downing Street, although no posters featuring Leete's

Lord Kitchener cartoon can be seen. They were donated by Mr R. Humphrey Davies C.B., who worked as a clerk to the Joint Recruiting Committee of the PRC.[26]

Copies of official minutes taken by Davies himself (also part of the BL collections) reveal that 'In 1915, the Committee was strengthened by the addition of 3 members of the Scottish Recruiting Committee and representatives of the Trades Union Congress and the Labour Party Committee, and was henceforward described as the Joint Recruiting Committee. The Committee met in the large Reception Room at 12 Downing Street (pictured on page 6), but two of its main sections met at Party Headquarters in St. Stephens Chambers... I

Below and across: Some posters used animals and children as emotional bribery.

can testify that throughout its proceedings, the Committee worked in the greatest harmony, taking care, at the same time, to ensure that it was a *voluntary effort* to secure recruits.'

A poster campaign of epic proportions

The PRC records reveal that the Sub-Department 'issued 164 posters of various shapes and sizes [all numbered 1 to 164], 10 cards for exhibition in windows, a large number of slips for use on taxi-cabs and trams and in railway carriages, long posters for use on gate posts in the country districts, and 65 pamphlets and leaflets varying in size from 56 paged pamphlets to single-paged leaflets. In the beginning the productions were circulated through the medium of the hundreds of Parliamentary Recruiting Committees throughout Great Britain, and by the aid of a large array of voluntary agencies.'[27]

Posters were developed using a wide range of formats and variety of psychological techniques to ensure their messages, both in letterpress and pictorial formats, were looked at, remembered and acted upon. Some posters forcefully projected imagery and words of demonisation, emasculation and emotional bribery. Happy, laughing, smiling and apparently fully satisfied soldiers were featured to entice new recruits.

Animals, children and women featured in designs to encourage men to enlist – notably in Arthur Wardle's THE EMPIRE NEEDS MEN! AUSTRALIA, CANADA, INDIA, NEW ZEALAND ALL ANSWER THE CALL. HELPED BY THE YOUNG LIONS THE OLD LION DEFIES HIS FOES. ENLIST NOW. The technique is also used in Savile Lumley's DADDY, WHAT DID <u>YOU</u> DO IN THE GREAT WAR? as well as in E.J. Kealey's

Daddy, what did _YOU_ do in the Great War?

E. J. KEALEY
WOMEN OF BRITAIN
SAY –
"GO!"
Published by the PARLIAMENTARY RECRUITING COMMITTEE, London. Poster No. 75
Printed by HILL, SIFFKEN & Co. (L.P.A. Ltd.), Grafton Works, London, N. W. 13741 25 M. 3/15

design declaring WOMEN OF BRITAIN SAY "GO!" Also, idyllic scenes of rural Britain, the homes of country and city folk as well as historic buildings were contrasted with both real and imagined images of devastation and ruins resulting from German bombing.

Even by modern standards the logistics were challenging and the statistics astonishing. The PRC records stated that 'From start to finish, the Sub-Department has printed and circulated 12,435,500 posters and taxi and tram slips; 450,000 window cards; 5,500,000 pamphlets; 34,125,000 leaflets and 1,750,000 miscellaneous productions. The quantity so produced reached the remarkable aggregate of 54,260,500 copies.' The cost of producing these copies was £40,489, according to PRC accounts. In addition, 'special attention was devoted to the local needs of London, Wales, Scotland and Ireland; and a number of posters and leaflets were issued in the Welsh language.'[28] The PRC records reveal that there was expenditure in terms of advertising, paper, printing, transportation and posting of the posters, although the government was eager to capitalise on free poster sites as far as possible. Davray revealed the impact in London of the PRC recruitment posters and also those produced by the Central

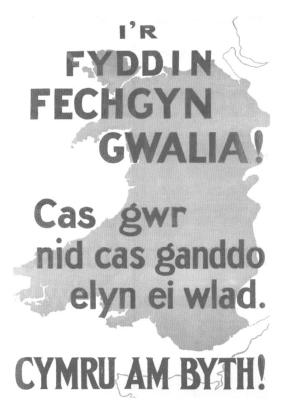

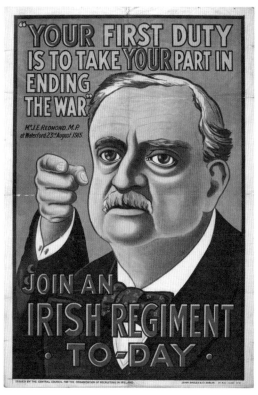

Above left: A Welsh language poster saying, 'To the Army, men of Gwalia! Hateful the man who hates not the enemy of his country. Wales for ever!' Above right: Rare Irish adaptation of the Kitchener design.

Across: Women were encouraged to back their men. Overleaf: 'Posters remind the crowd that the country is fighting for its independence' – Davray.

London Recruiting Depot. He observed the wide range of formats, shapes and sizes of the posters that were utilised individually and collectively for maximum impact and effect: 'A complete organisation for publicity and bill-sticking has been evolved; the bills are distributed and pasted up in millions. They are of all shapes and sizes – handbills, demy bills, long horizontal bands, narrow placards, and panels several yards high.'

He continued: 'They are of the most varied descriptions, and it would need a volume at least to describe them all. We will merely describe a few of the most characteristic. A frame of red, white and blue, the royal arms with the French mottoes: "*Dieu et mon droit*" and "*Honi soit qui mal y pense*" between the initials "G.R."; below, in blue letters, a statement, signed by the King, to the effect that: We are fighting for a noble purpose, and we will not lay down our arms until that purpose has been achieved – followed by this appeal in capital letters: "Men of the Empire. To arms!" and, under a blue line, in blue letters: "God save the King!"… A little further on, a facsimile of the seals and signatures appended to the treaty of 1839 which guaranteed the neutrality of Belgium is accompanied by this commentary: "Germany has trampled under foot the treaty which she had signed. Will Britons stand on one side while Germany destroys an innocent nation?"'

Davray proceeded to describe larger posters: 'On the Corinthian portico of the Mansion House, the official residence of the Lord Mayor, an inscription in enormous letters on two immense posters reminds the crowd which, from morning to evening surges in front of the Royal Exchange and the Bank that the country is fighting for its independence.'

And provide details of further posters: 'On the bridge at Ludgate Hill is displayed the following appeal: "The Empire is at stake. Rally round the flag"; and, as you walk down Fleet Street, the home of the Press and more crowded than the Rue Montmartre, or as you come out of St. Paul's Cathedral, or as you come from Blackfriars and the right bank of the river, or by Farringdon Street from Holborn or the great provision markets, this legend meets your eye and forces itself upon your attention. In the West End it is the same thing as in the City. On the fronts of the great hotels, from top to bottom, inscriptions on calico, strongly framed, repeat, in letters a yard high, that England is counting on the support of all her children.'

Britain benefitted from having the most advanced advertising industry outside of the USA. In 1914, 'the advertising industry was remarkably large and buoyantly confident. Annual expenditure on advertising approached £100 million… about half this huge budget, perhaps £40–£50 million, was spent placing advertisements in newspapers and magazines, and guaranteed the livelihood of some 240 general advertising agencies in London alone.'[29]

The advertisers were used to competing for attention outdoors and within spacious interiors. In incremental order, their sizes ranged from 4-sheet (40 x 60 inches) to 48-sheet (120 x 240 inches). Additional standard sizes now include 64-sheet and 96-sheet posters, and larger sizes of various formats were used during the war years. At the other end of the scale, many of the PRC posters measured only 30 x 20 inches, and so this meant that PRC designs (and privately-printed posters too) had to be grouped together to obtain eye-catching effects, especially in outdoor settings.

Come into the ranks and fight for your King and Country—Don't stay in the crowd and stare

YOU ARE WANTED AT · THE · FRONT

ENLIST TO·DAY

PUBLISHED BY THE PARLIAMENTARY RECRUITING COMMITTEE, LONDON · POSTER No 74

QUEEN MARY'S
ARMY AUXILIARY
CORPS.
WE'RE LOOKING
TO YOU
TO JOIN OUR
CIRCLE!
ENROL TO-DAY
FULL PARTICULARS AND FORMS OF
APPLICATION FROM THE NEAREST
EMPLOYMENT EXCHANGE.
ASK AT POST OFFICE FOR ADDRESS.
M 40/59.

However, the smaller poster sizes did work well in other public settings and spaces such as clubs, hotels, pubs, restaurants and shops.

In order to display the posters, more and more women were encouraged to take the place of men who had either volunteered or were conscripted in 1916. W.E.D. Allen recorded the experiences of 'one of the first of these adventuresses, who went into billposting even before the passing of the Conscription Act'. She wrote: 'Most people think billposting a queer job for a woman, but I was tired of being in a corset factory and wanted outdoor work… I had to practise a long time before I could use a paste brush and post a bill properly. A poster that is covered with paste is as bad as sticky fly-paper to get mixed up with. Then I had to learn the different kinds of posters received from the printers, and how to sort and fold them, and the way to load a van.'

She continued: 'I had two months' training before going my first round without a man to superintend, but we girls have now been going out by ourselves for about six weeks. We go in motor or horse vans in parties of three – one to drive and two to post. Handling the ladders is rather awkward, but specially light ones are given to us. Special uniforms – dark overalls, divided skirts, and black water-proof sou'wester hats – are provided so I am all right for climbing ladders, and I have worked so high as twenty feet up. It was rather giddy work at first, but luckily I have not dropped a paste pot on anybody's head yet. I have been chaffed and laughed at a good deal, but have to put up with that, though I sometimes feel I should like to give those who jeer a dab with the paste brush. I am only keeping things going until the war is over, and am not doing any man out of a job, so I get on very well with the men billposters. We

Above: A Norfolk girl putting up recruitment posters.

women can post what is called a 32-sheet bill, that is about ten feet by thirteen feet, made up of smaller sheets.'

A black and white photograph by Horace Nicholls, who worked for the government during World War I in the Imperial War Museum, depicted a girl in 1918 from the Norfolk town of Thetford up a ladder at work with brush– and paste, continuing her father's work as Official Bill Poster and Town Crier. One of the posters in the photograph promotes Queen Mary's Army Auxiliary Corps. It depicts a woman with outstretched arm and pointing finger, a rare adaptation of Leete's cartoon design.

The Women's Army Auxiliary Corps (WAAC) was formed in January 1917 and recruited the first women into the British Army to serve in a non-nursing capacity. The WAAC provided catering, storekeeping, vehicle maintenance and clerical duties for the British Army, freeing more men to take up combat

Above: Lucy Kemp-Welch's 'Forward'.
Across: Poster inspired by the sinking of the *Lusitania*.

roles. In 1918, Queen Mary became patron and the corps was renamed Queen Mary's Army Auxiliary Corps. Over 57,000 women enrolled in the WAAC / QMAAC during World War I and though they were not given full military status, the women often worked close to the frontline. Three military medals were awarded to members for gallantry. The QMAAC was eventually disbanded in September 1921.

In terms of how the vast body of material, in particular posters, was commissioned and created, the PRC revealed that it was 'inundated by suggestions and designs from various printing firms (who usually engaged the services of their in-house artists) and from individuals and each was carefully considered. A few ideas were accepted outright, while several were utilised with modification either of the details in drawing, colouring or wording. Many were created by the Committee itself.' Also, 'Realising that the struggle would be a long and stern one, the aim of the Department throughout was to issue posters that would stimulate and not depress. It took its key note from the splendid spirit of the soldiers themselves and it set its face resolutely against depicting scenes of a gruesome character.'[30]

There was no single person responsible for co-ordinating the poster campaigns, and this was a fundamental problem with the PRC. Hedley Le Bas was a significant adviser but he was not given overall control. In the absence of a guiding hand it was inevitable that a reactive rather than pro-active style of management would develop via a series of committees, and sometimes this was all too evident in the designs of the posters.

Occasionally the PRC would benefit from artists coming forward themselves to offer their services, but this was infrequent and the majority of posters were created anonymously. The PRC was 'fortunate to be able to avail itself of the voluntary services of such well-known artists as the Misses Edith and Lucy Kemp-Welch, whose "REMEMBER SCARBOROUGH" and "FORWARD" will be remembered as two of the most striking posters. Mr Bernard Partridge, the famous

Punch cartoonist, depicted, in the "Take up the Sword of Justice" design, the sinking of the *Lusitania*. On 7th May 1915, this Cunard ocean liner had been sunk by German torpedoes as it approached Ireland. She was carrying some American citizens and later this encouraged the USA to break its official isolationist policy and enter the war as an 'associate power', giving Britain much-needed support.

The PRC accounts, under a special section entitled 'Influence of The Productions', listed the most popular posters by the volume of demand:

LORD KITCHENER, Nos. 113 and 117: 145,000
REMEMBER BELGIUM, Nos. 16 and 19: 140,000
TAKE UP THE SWORD OF JUSTICE, Nos. 105, 106 and 111: 105,000
TO SERVE THE GUNS, Nos. 85, A, B and C: 101,000
HE DID HIS DUTY. WILL YOU DO YOURS?, (Lord Roberts), No. 20: 95,000
COME ALONG, BOYS! No. 22: 92,000
FALL IN, Nos. 12 and 13: 85,000
THE VETERAN'S FAREWELL, Nos. 24 and 63: 71,500
LINE UP BOYS, No. 54: 65,000
ENGLAND EXPECTS, No. 101: 60,000
FOLLOW ME! No. 11: 55,000
AT THE FRONT, No. 84: 55,000
OUR FLAG, No. 107: 40,000

The PRC added: 'Of necessity, the King's Message (in poster form), which opened up a much wider field of activity, had a vast circulation, 290,000 copies being distributed.'[31]

Hiley has compiled a more detailed list incorporating additional data resulting in a top fifteen of PRC posters. They are arranged in order of popularity:

1   LORD KITCHENER. Photograph of Lord Kitchener, with text from the speech, including 'Does The Call Of Duty Find No Response In You Until Reinforced… By The Call Of Compulsion?' Printed by David Allen and Sons, circa July to August 1915, as posters PRC 113 (20 x 30 inches) and PRC 117 (40 x 50 inches). Numbers printed: 145,000.

2   REMEMBER BELGIUM – ENLIST TO-DAY. In the official description: 'a British soldier on guard in the foreground whilst in the background a woman and her babes are in flight from a blazing home'. Designed and printed by Henry Jenkinson Ltd, circa December 1914 to March 1915, as PRC 16 (40 x 30 inches) and PRC 19 (20 x 15 inches). Number printed: 140,000.

3   TAKE UP THE SWORD OF JUSTICE. The sinking of the *Lusitania* with a figure rising from

TAKE UP THE SWORD OF JUSTICE

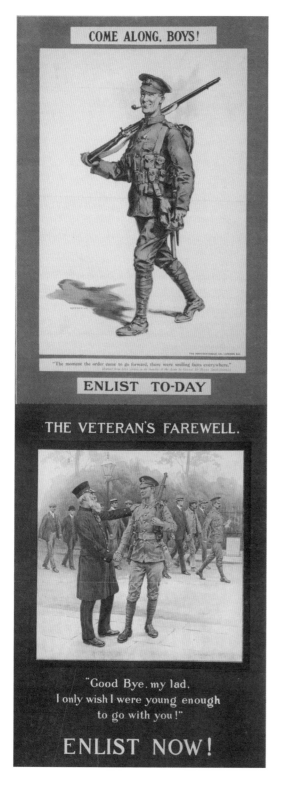

the sea and offering a sword. Printed by David Allen and Sons, Harrow, September 1915, as PRC 105 (40 x 25 inches), PRC 106 (60 x 40 inches) and PRC 111 (30 x 20 inches). Number printed: 105,000.

4   WE'RE BOTH NEEDED TO SERVE THE GUNS! FILL UP THE RANKS! PILE UP THE MUNITIONS!. A soldier and munitions worker shaking hands with a battle scene in the background. Commissioned by the PRC, apparently at the request of the War Office and printed by Chorley and Pickersgill Ltd, circa May 1915, as posters PRC 85a (probably 80 x 120 inches), 85b (40 x 50 inches) and 85c (20 x 30 inches). Number printed: 101,000.

5   HE DID HIS DUTY. WILL YOU DO YOURS?. Portrait of Lord Roberts with his Victoria Cross and symbols of office. Printed by Johnson, Riddle and Co, circa December 1914, as PRC 20 (30 x 20 inches). There is also a Welsh version of this poster. Number printed: 95,000.

6   COME ALONG BOYS! ENLIST TO-DAY. A smiling soldier with a quotation from Sir Horace Smith-Dorrien: 'The moment the order came to go forward, there were smiling faces everywhere'. Designed and printed by The Haycock-Cadle Co, and initially released circa November 1914 as the PRC's first 'window-card', PRC 100c (11 x 11 inches). Also printed by the same company, circa December 1914 to January 1915, as poster PRC 22 (30 x 20 inches). The company also printed a Welsh version, and issued its design in a large poster

Above left: 'Come Along Boys! Enlist To-Day!'

Left: 'The Veteran's Farewell'.

The hugely popular 'Remember Belgium'.

Above: Part of Nelson's famous signal used on an official poster. Across: 'Line Up, Boys! Enlist To-Day'.

for the Central London Recruiting Depot. Number printed: 92,000.

7 "Fall In" Answer Now In Your Country's Hour Of Need. A bugler is blowing a call. Designed and printed by Hill, Siffken and Co., circa November 1914 as posters PRC 12 (30 x 20 inches) and 13 (size unknown). The company also used its design in a large poster for the Central London Recruiting Depot. Number printed: 85,000.

8 The Veteran's Farewell. "Good Bye, my lad, I only wish I were young enough to go with you!" ENLIST NOW! Initially designed by Frank Dadd (an artist who worked for *The Graphic* magazine) as a tobacco advertisement and subsequently used as a recruiting poster 'by Kind Permission of Messrs. Abdulla & Co. Ltd', and printed by both Straker Bros and by Petty and Sons, with a first release circa December 1914 and a reissue circa February 1915. Numbered PRC 24 (sepia, 30 x 20 inches) and renumbered as PRC 63s

on reissue. The colour version was numbered PRC 63 (30 x 20 inches). Number printed: 71,500.

9 Line Up, Boys! Enlist To-day. Four kilted soldiers marching side by side. Apparently designed by Eyre and Spottiswoode, who were described as 'owners of the copyright'. Printed by them and by A.White and Co. circa January to April 1915 as poster PRC 54 (30 x 20 inches). Number printed: 65,000.

10 Lads, you're wanted: Go And Help. Advancing soldiers in silhouette. Printed by David Allen and Sons, circa March to May 1915, as poster PRC 78 (6 x 30 inches). Number printed: at least 65,000.

11 1805 "England Expects" 1915. Portrays Lord Nelson and the sea with the strapline 'Are YOU Doing YOUR Duty To-day?'. Apparently designed by Seargeant Bros, who added 'Design Copyright' to the imprint. Printed by them, circa May 1915 as PRC 101 (20 x 30 inches) with the design later reissued as a poster for the Publicity Department, Admiralty Recruiting Office. Number printed: 60,000.

12 If you cannot join the army – Try & get a Recruit. White letterpress poster on a red and blue background. Printed by Haycock-Cadle Co., circa December to March 1915, as poster PRC 32 (30 x 20 inches). Number printed: at least 60,000.

13 Follow me! Your Country Needs YOU. A marching soldier. This poster design is by E.J. Kealey (probably Edward J. Kealey

LINE UP, BOYS!

ENLIST TO-DAY.

Published by the Parliamentary Recruiting Committee, London.   Poster No. 54.   [W. 422/405   20m. 4/15. F. & S. Ltd.

BRITONS!

YOUR COUNTRY NEEDS YOU.

Published by the PARLIAMENTARY RECRUITING COMMITTEE, LONDON.—Poster No. 22. Wt. 9956. 50M.   Printed by SAUNDERS & CULLINGHAM, 2 & 3 Burgon Street, Carter Lane, London, E.C. 1632/12/14.

and sometimes mistakenly written as E.V. Keeley), an artist who worked for Hill, Siffken and Co. Printed circa November to December 1914 as poster PRC 11 (30 x 20 inches). Number printed: 55,000.

14 At The Front! Every fit Briton should join our brave men at the Front. Enlist Now. Showing a field gun team and shellbursts. Printed by E.S. and A. Robinson Ltd, circa April 1915 as poster PRC 84 (30 x 20 inches). Number printed: 55,000.

15 Britons! Your Country Needs YOU. Red lettering over grey map of Great Britain and Ireland. Printed by Saunders and Cullingham in December 1914 as poster PRC 23 (30 x 20 inches). Number printed: at least 50,000.

New ideas: outdoor meetings, Highland bands and Pals battalions

The display of posters went hand-in-hand with many other recruitment activities. As the war progressed new plans were developed and implemented. According to the PRC minutes 'it was resolved to adhere to the method of simultaneous meetings, to give each district a big scheme of outdoor gatherings and to cover the whole country. From some of the large centres such as Manchester and Liverpool, Leicester and Bristol it was resolved to organise a large number of meetings each night for the surrounding districts. Several new and attractive methods were put into operation. At Huddersfield, Leeds, Halifax, Bradford and other large cities the municipalities provided brilliantly decorated and illuminated tramcars, which, accompanied bands and speakers, were run out to various centres where, using the cars as a platform, most successful meetings were held.

'In other large cities such as Nottingham, Newcastle and Birmingham, permanent outdoor platforms were erected in market squares and open spaces at which recruiting meetings were held daily and in some cases all day. Bands formed an attractive feature at these meetings and great crowds gathered. Recruiting officers, medical officers and magistrates were in attendance to enrol recruits on the spot; and on the same day or the day following, the new recruits were marched off to the station or to the depot, headed by military bands playing patriotic airs.'[32]

Edward George Villiers Stanley (1865–1948), better known by his title Lord Derby, served as British Minister of War from 1916 to 1918. He was a Conservative who joined Asquith's wartime coalition government and introduced new schemes to encourage recruits. His proposal of 'Pals battalions' derived from an earlier idea of General Sir Henry Rawlinson. Lord Kitchener approved it. The idea was that groups of men from the same walks of life with shared work or leisure pursuits could serve together. Administrators, clerks, bank workers – men from the same factory and football team could join and fight together.

By the end of September 1914, over fifty towns had formed Pals battalions, whilst the larger towns and cities were able to form several battalions. Notable among them were 'Pals' from Accrington, Birmingham, Bradford, Durham, Grimsby, Liverpool, Lothian, Manchester, Newcastle, Salford and Sheffield. The scheme was in part positive as it ensured that men were motivated by being surrounded by friends who shared the same interests. A serious negative was that entire communities could be wiped out.

One of the most effective means of recruitment was the use of Highland bands. The PRC records stated: 'Perhaps the most successful piece of work carried out by the Sub-division of the PRC in this direction was undertaken by Lieutenant W J West and his Highland Pipe Band. This band, consisting of twelve members, toured the country from Cornwall to Northumberland, and its record whether in town or country was one unending triumph for voluntary effort. The campaign commenced on November 22nd 1914 and concluded on February 26th 1916. The band has worked from the following centres:

'Ashford, Barnsley, Bolton, Boston, Bourne, Bradford, Canterbury, Camborne, Chatham, Congleton, Consett, Dartford, Durham, Deal, Grays, Gravesend, Hastings, Helston, Huddersfield, Keighley, Leeds, Loughborough, Leicester, Macclesfield, Maidstone, Margate, Nelson, Penistone, Redruth, Rochdale, Sleaford, Southend, Sittingbourne, Spalding, Truro, Woking and Wilmslow.

'Altogether 651 towns, cities and villages were visited. The following figures are interesting:

'Miles travelled by railway 22,201
Miles marched 3,439
Speeches made by Lieut. West 859
… Recruits gained 22,201

'The War Office engaged Lauder's Highland Band for several weeks… the new plan of carrying the campaign into the open air had an immediate effect upon recruiting, and in many districts recruiting officers informed us that the numbers equalled, and in some cases exceeded, the recruits enrolled in the first few weeks of the war.'[33]

Sir Henry Lauder, known professionally as Harry Lauder, was an international Scottish entertainer, described by Sir Winston Churchill as 'Scotland's greatest ever ambassador!' Private Joseph Quigley's charming, comically illustrated publication *The Slogan – Side-Lights on Recruiting: with Harry Lauder's Band* (Simpkin, Marshall, Hamilton, Kent & Co., Ltd, London, 1916) highlighted the importance of the band's work, which included a nine-week tour of Scotland: 'what other band could sound the slogan in the World War but a band of pipers? Wherever Scottish regiments have set their faces to the foe, the shrill, defiant notes of the pibroch have been the talisman that revived the spirits of sinking men, made the long, weary march over hill and desert more lightsome, transmuted dark despair to glowing hope, and turned many a well-nigh hopeless field to imperishable victory. Wherever Scotsmen are, the straight and certain way to their hearts is along that avenue… which their national music can alone provide.

And, 'With this knowledge, the Bands Bureau, which had been formed in Glasgow to supply musicians to bandless battalions, evolved the idea of sending out a company of pipers who would bear the Fiery Cross throughout the length and breadth of Scotland. The Central Recruiting Committee received the proposal with favour, and the War Office extended its benediction… Mr Harry Lauder consented to give his name to the band, which achieved an immediate success under the direction of Mr Joseph Quigley, the Honorary Manager of the Bands Bureau, who had been requested to undertake the organisation and management of the tour.'

YOUR COUNTRY'S CALL

Isn't this worth fighting for?

ENLIST NOW

PUBLISHED BY THE PARLIAMENTARY RECRUITING COMMITTEE, LONDON. POSTER Nº 67.

PRINTED BY JOWETT & SOWRY, LEEDS.

The band was invited across the border and, when marching towards Bradford in West Yorkshire, Quigley noted that 'The girls had discovered something more entertaining than work. A full highland pipe band was a real novelty… here as in many other parts of England numerous girls pleased for small pieces of the bright tartan kilt as a keepsake… It may have been nothing more than coincidence, but at the end of the tour the inside folds of several kilts had shrunk considerably… and it certainly suggested that had the tour lasted much longer the Band, or some members of it, would have played their farewell march in tunic and a sporran.'

Henry Davray also observed the Highland bands in London: 'Here are the Scotch; the bagpipes fill the air with their shrill music; the men are superb; their high white gaiters move lightly up and down, and at every step, their pleated kilts expand like opening fans. An instant later, in some open space – Trafalgar Square, St. Paul's churchyard, Covent Garden, or one of the Circuses – a band strikes up; the musicians blow in their little short bugles, to the notes of which succeed the piercing fifes, backed up by drums; the drumsticks rain down blows on the parchment, while one energetic performer, enveloped in a vast leather apron, deals vigorous alternate strokes on the big drum.'

The decline of the recruitment poster

PRC records outlined the ebb and flow of the work rate of the Publications Sub-Department: 'Work was great until temporary suspension in July 1915 and then continued in middle of September... and the SD proceeded to prepare a further batch of pictorial appeals.' At the beginning of October, however, Lord Derby (the newly appointed Director General of Recruiting) intimated his opinion that pictorial posters had had their day. It was decided to complete the printing of the half dozen posters which remained in the press, but from that time forward the number of picture posters was restricted and eventually curtailed.

'The issue of His Majesty the King's message to His People marked a new stage in the SD's work, and from that time onward the volume of the publications was very great indeed. Save for a lull in December 1915 the Publications Department was engaged at high pressure... With the passing of the Military Services Act there came a recrudescence of activity; but by the month of April 1916 the work of the Department had sunk to its minimum.'

What exactly did Lord Derby mean by asserting that 'pictorial posters had had their day'? There is evidence of a growing resentment among soldiers of the recruitment posters. The cumulative effects of the 'bullying by

Across and below: Reminding men of their duty to fight, both David Allen and Sons posters, 1915.

poster' were producing detrimental effects to the war effort and 'by the end of July 1915 the War Office begged the PRC to suspend operations arguing that its target market was now clearly "sick of posters and recruitment meetings"' and by 'the end of September 1915 official confidence in the poster campaign had in fact evaporated'.[34]

Initially patriotism played a part in the soldiers' reluctance to relay the real horrors of war back home. Their mail was censored too. However, as the war went on, real reports were circulated back home and they made a stark contrast to the idealised images of war service projected by many of the recruitment posters. With very few exceptions British posters specifically avoided images of death, dreadful injuries and disablement. However, some artists provided psychological insights into the horrific effects of war. One oil painting, entitled 'Return To The Front: Victoria Railway Station' (1916), is now part of the York Art Gallery collections. The Sunderland-born artist Richard Jack (1866–1952) had studied art in York, London and Paris.

In 1916, Jack received a commission from the Canadian War Memorials Fund and was sent to northern France, serving with the rank of Major with a Canadian regiment; this was at the instigation of Sir Max Aitken, later Lord Beaverbrook. The artist was sent to France, attached to the Headquarters of General Sir Arthur Currie, to enable him to collect first-hand data and sketches for the two vast canvases (just over 12 x 20 feet) he was to paint in London: 'The Second Battle of Ypres – April

Richard Jack's 'Return to the Front: Victoria Railway Station'.

22nd to May 25th, 1915' and 'The Taking of Vimy Ridge, Easter Monday'. These were exhibited at a joint exhibition of Canadian and British War Records at the Royal Academy of Arts in London before they were shipped to Canada, where they now hang in the collection at the Canadian War Museum, Ottawa.

Many of the now celebrated wartime pictures and sculptures were displayed at the Royal Academy (the most prestigious arts organisation in Britain) during and immediately after the war. They were commissioned as part of various official art schemes, and were featured for propaganda, commemorative and fundraising purposes. Among the famous names were: Muirhead Bone, Francis Dodd, George Clausen, Jacob Epstein, Stanhope Forbes, Charles Sargeant Jagger, Augustus John, Eric Kennington, John Lavery, Percy Wyndham Lewis, John and Paul Nash, C.R.W. Nevinson, William Orpen, Charles Pears, John Singer Sargent, Stanley Spencer, Philip Wilson Steer and Norman Wilkinson.

In 'Return To The Front', Jack captured the disillusionment of soldiers at the railway station. Only one can be seen smiling. The Scottish soldier seated on the floor close to the girl selling copies of popular magazines (which may well have included *The Bystander*, *London Opinion* and *Punch*) is lost in thought about his family and his future. To that end Jack created, although almost certainly unintentionally, what appears to modern eyes to be an anti-war picture. It was exhibited by Jack in a private capacity at the Royal Academy in 1916. Jack was a popular and versatile artist who painted portraits of King George V and Queen Mary, he became a Royal Academician (RA) in 1920 and emigrated to Canada in 1938.

Dwindling public enthusiasm for recruitment posters reached a tipping point in the early summer months of 1915. Production far exceeded the demand for the PRC posters, and stockpiling turned from being a frustration into a scandal that leaked into the public domain. The problems of tens of thousands of posters in storage prompted cartoon parodies, one of which appeared in *The Bystander* on 8th September 1915, entitled 'What to Do with Our War Posters – A Hint To Advertisers showing how, if the war were to end suddenly, the surplus stock of recruiting posters left on the country's hands could be usefully turned to account'.[35]

Both letterpress and pictorial types of poster would continue to be produced during the war years, but in considerably smaller numbers. PRC records demonstrated that posters had played a crucial role (albeit, in some quarters, an unpopular and unwelcome one) in the enlistment of men for active service and women for work on the Home Front, from the outbreak of World War I until the end of summer in 1915. Posters had been part-and-parcel of a global operation of influence.

The writer of the article 'Recruiting By Poster' (*Windsor Magazine* No. 246, June 1915) – who probably worked on behalf of the PRC, so the content needs to be treated with a degree of caution – noted that 'The hoardings of the country have been covered with an infinite variety of pictorial and letterpress appeals to the manhood of the nation to come forward and take a share in that greatest of all fights, the struggle for national existence.

'The magnitude of this modern auxiliary to the efforts of the recruiting-sergeant has had the effect of attracting widespread criticism. Some sensitive folk seem to think it very sad that a

great country should find it necessary to resort to what has been stigmatised as "bullying by poster". But what alternative would they suggest? It is scarcely possible that the exhibition of millions of posters can have failed to produce useful results. It is manifestly impossible to gauge the influence which has been exerted by this medium: yet it is a reasonable assumption that a goodly percentage of those who have joined the military forces since the outbreak of the Great War have been directly influenced, if not entirely led, by the Parliamentary Recruiting Committee's publications.'

The article also revealed that 'Natives of Holland and other neutral States on the Continent have asked for copies of posters, and there have been applications from France and Russia. From the United States also numerous letters have been received, and from many parts of the British empire have emanated requests for supplies – from Canada, Newfoundland, British Colombia, India, Australasia, and South Africa, and from others of the Colonies, and an exceedingly interesting fact is that specific illustrations have found their way to the Australian camp under the shadow of the Pyramids in Egypt. What more convincing proof could be wished of the world-wide influence of this remarkable poster campaign?'

The PRC proudly boasted that 'the work was not by any means confined to the Mother country. From all parts of the Empire and from various neutral countries came requests for supplies [of posters]… it is a fair assumption that there is hardly a civilised part of the globe to which our publications have not found their way. In Canada and in Australia [they have made] important use of our posters and pamphlets… aiding the Recruitment

Movement… and many tons of them have been shipped across the Atlantic in the last few months.'[36]

However, the protracted war on several fronts had required increasing numbers of manpower (let's not forget the womanpower needed in many other spheres of operation too), and by the end of summer 1915 the introduction of conscription was viewed by many as inevitable. Rather than disband the machinery of the PRC, it was later transformed into the Parliamentary War Savings Committee.

Across: Posters showing laughing and happy soldiers caused resentment once the true horrors of war became known.

Below: McCaw, Stevenson & Orr's Irish recruitment poster produced in Belfast and Dublin.

CHAPTER 3

ALFRED LEETE'S LIFE AND ACHIEVEMENTS

AND THE BIRTH OF THE LONDON SKETCH CLUB

Alfred Ambrose Chew Leete was born on 28th August 1882 in the historic village of Thorpe Achurch, near Northampton in the east Midlands of England. Known as 'A' by his family, he was the eldest child of John Alfred Leete and Harriet Eliza, née Chew. His father came from a long line of farmers that can be traced back to the Norman Conquest.

Leete had two brothers, John and Sidney, as well as a sister, Sarah Frances. In 1893, the whole family moved from Northamptonshire to the seaside town of Weston-super-Mare on the west coast of Somerset, close to the city of Bristol, where it was hoped that the fresh air and warmer weather would be beneficial to his father's ill-health. Farming life was left behind and his parents established a thriving hotel business, which included Addington House and Sutherland House. Leete would later spend a considerable amount of time in London maintaining a house there, although he regarded Weston-super-Mare as his adopted home.[37]

Alfred Leete attended Kingsholme School and went on

Above: Alfred Leete self-portrait.
Across: Leete's cartoon for his home town.

to the School of Science and Art. Sadly, his sister Sarah died, but two younger siblings, Hilda and Dorothy, completed the family.

Family records show that Leete was interested in drawing from an early age and his father arranged for Leete to take up an apprenticeship with a Bristol architect. In those days, draughtsmanship was a fundamental part of that profession. Leete was bored with the work but it helped to improve his artistic skills and develop his knowledge of perspective. He was encouraged by his employer, who also practised as an artist and contributed drawings to local magazines, including *Bristol Magpie*. An example of Leete's early work for that magazine was published in the Christmas edition of 1902. It depicted, in the popular linear Art Nouveau style of the time, a fashionable lady raising a glass of champagne. The design is accompanied by the caption 'Wishing You a Merry Xmas', and signed with his initials A.L. From the 1910s, he would introduce his trademark 'dropped T' signature.[38]

Life as a commercial artist

Adventure and ambition were no doubt behind Leete's decision to leave the architect's office and head for London, hopeful that the newspapers and magazines based in and close to Fleet Street would pay handsomely for his artwork. His youthful optimism was temporarily dampened by the large number of rejections, and he returned to Bristol to work as a designer in a furniture factory.

However, Leete had a positive outlook on life. By all accounts he was a genial and witty man. The author and historian Lornie Leete-Hodge, perhaps best known for *The Country Life Book of Diana, Princess of Wales* (Book

Club Associates, 1982), wrote a small catalogue to accompany an exhibition about her forebear held at the Woodspring Museum, Weston-super-Mare, in 1985. She believed him to be possessed of three essential qualities: 'perseverance, prolific output and popular manner – "A" determined to make good through the days of the Boer War – [of] great hardship and unemployment, but he did not give up, and at last the editor of *Ally Sloper* magazine took some of his work at five shillings each.'[39]

The full title of this weekly magazine was *Ally Sloper's Half-Holiday* and this British comic, first published on 3rd May 1884, has a legitimate claim to being the first comic magazine named after and featuring a regular character. Ally Sloper was a good-for-nothing lazy schemer often in trouble and invariably found 'sloping' in alleyways to escape his landlord and other creditors. The magazine was published at The Sloperies, Bolt Court in Fleet Street, London. According to Leete-Hodge, her famous ancestor's feet were finally on the career ladder.

Leete may well have contributed to some magazines before Ally Sloper. Jim Aulich's biography of Leete for the *Oxford Dictionary of National Biography* noted that 'As a self-taught artist his first paid work came in 1897 when the *Daily Graphic* accepted one of his drawings. He also contributed to the *Bristol Magpie* before moving in 1899 to London, where he took up a post as an artist with a printer.'

Alfred Leete usually drew his cartoons, although he would also use watercolours and was versatile enough to paint any subject, according to Leete-Hodge. She recalled 'A torn scrapbook from a holiday in France, not even dated, [that] shows a galaxy of sketches of people and places his keen eye had observed and re-created. There are old men, women, places such as Grasse where he has captured a corner house with flowered balcony; elegant Monaco with the Prince's yacht; the Cathedral at Dijon (not the building as such as the gargoyles around it); the Rhone ferry boat, an address in Nice; but for fashionable Nice itself, that haven of English tourists, he chooses an old French washerwoman lumbering up the shore, a basket of washing on her head. The book is signed, of course, with a caricatured self-portrait complete with small dog.'

Leete occasionally painted in oils but he never considered himself to be a fine artist. He took great pride, derived enormous satisfaction and earned a good living, from practising as a cartoonist, comic illustrator and commercial artist. His wealth at death in 1933 was the considerable sum of £9,579 6s. 3d.

Leete's advertising and commercial work included artwork for local businesses in his beloved Weston-super-Mare, but also for many national companies, such as Bovril, Connolly Leather (supplying primarily to car

manufacturers), Guinness, Hector Powe (an English tailoring company), Pratt's Petrol, Rowntree's chocolates, Ronuk Polish and Younger's Brewery. He is credited with devising the 'Father William' character (who had a distinctive, long, white beard) for William Younger's Brewery, and 'Mr York of York, Yorks', who 'recommends Rowntree's Plain York Chocolate', both creations of the 1920s.[40]

From 1915 to 1928, he supplied artwork for the Underground Electric Railway Company, the precursor to the London Underground. One memorable example, 'The Lure of The Underground' (1927), depicted people in London (all wearing hats) being drawn down into the Underground system by a mysterious force. The image is one of the most popular sellers in the Museum of Transport shop in Covent Garden and can be found on fridge magnets, mugs and notebooks. Leete was personally proud of 'The Roads Are Never Up On The London Underground', printed in 1928, and the original artwork featured on the wall in the background of a photograph depicting Leete working at his desk. Leete submitted drawings, cartoons and illustrations for advertising and to illustrate topical news events, for stand-alone humorous sketches, and for the covers of many of the leading magazines of the day, including: *Illustrated London News*, *Punch*, *Strand Magazine*, *Tatler*, *The Bystander*, *The Passing Show* and *The Sketch*. *Pick Me Up* ran his series 'Play Titles Travestied' from 1899 to 1907, and it was then continued in *London Opinion*. *Punch* first published one of his cartoons on 22nd November 1905 and last published one on 28th October 1931. Leete also benefitted from regular commissions from the *Pall Mall Gazette* and this additional security encouraged him to propose to Edith Jane, the daughter of William Webb, who was an accountant. They were married on 7th November 1909. Their surviving child, a son, was born in 1915.

In good company with A.E. Johnson and the London Sketch Club

Freelancing in commercial art was a precarious means of employment, however, Leete was developing a valuable network of contacts and also representation from the artists' agent A.E. Johnson, an association established prior to his marriage. The Somerset Heritage Centre has a collection of Leete's work that includes references to A.E. Johnson. On the back of a drawing entitled 'Breaking it Gently' (circa 1910), depicting a man tying to break open

an egg, can be found the following details: 'Return to A.E. Johnson, Artists' Agent, 10 Lancaster Place, W.C., London.'

According to English Company Records, A.E. Johnson had incorporated his business on 1st January 1900 and it was still active in the early 1960s. Johnson himself was a former journalist and writer who penned a series of books, entitled *Brush, Pen and Pencil*, promoting the work of artists who worked predominantly in black and white. They included John Hassall in 1907 followed by (in alphabetical order): Tom Browne, Dudley Hardy, Frank Reynolds, William Heath Robinson (the devisor of wacky gadgets and machines) and Lawson Wood, known for his humorous depictions of animals, especially the ginger ape called Gran'pop. Some proved so popular they were reprinted in the 1930s.

Henry Mayo Bateman, famous for his 'The Man Who...' series, which featured comically exaggerated reactions to minor and usually upper-class social gaffes, was among the notable artists, cartoonists and illustrators on the books of A.E. Johnson. There was also Bruce Bairnsfather; the *Punch* contributors Frank Reynolds, Ernest Shepard, W.A. Sillince and Norman Thelwell; the marine painter Frank Henry Mason; sporting artist Lionel Edwards; and landscape painter Edward Seago.

Bairnsfather was popularly known for his humorous series of drawings showing life in the trenches for *The Bystander*. It featured 'Old Bill', the curmudgeonly Tommy with trademark walrus moustache and balaclava, and it brilliantly captured the absurdity of war on the Western Front. His work was drawn from first-hand experience having joined the Royal Warwickshire Regiment in 1914 in which he served with a machine gun unit in France until 1915. The cartoons were extremely popular with serving soldiers

Across: 'HMS Lion'.
Top: 'Breaking it Gently'.
Right: 'Help'.

because although they were exaggerated for comic effect they also caught realistic aspects of the hardships of the trenches.

Bairnsfather, Bateman and Mason also created posters themselves, or their images were incorporated into propaganda designs, during both World Wars. Cyril Kenneth Bird, better known by the pseudonym 'Fougasse', was also represented by A.E. Johnson. He started working for *Punch* during World War I and became art editor and later editor of the magazine. He created the celebrated series of anti-rumour and gossip posters entitled 'Careless Talk Costs Lives', first printed in February 1940.[41]

Although Leete did mingle and socialise with fine artists (painters in watercolours and oils who exhibited at the official societies), 'he shunned the traditional art establishment and once famously remarked that he "would rather win a medal at golf than be an RA [Royal Academician]," according to Leete-Hodge.

Leete was at home in the confines of clubs, especially those frequented by commercial artists, cartoonists and illustrators. He was a prominent member of the London Sketch Club, which was founded in 1898. Today, members still meet weekly 'for life drawing, conviviality and supper, carrying on the traditions of the artist members'. Originally, members were part of the Langham Sketching Club, but 'in 1898 a ridiculous argument broke out amongst its members, as to whether the suppers should be hot or cold. Daft as it may seem now, a largish group including such luminaries as Cecil Aldin, Tom Browne, Dudley Hardy, John Hassall and Phil May, who all wanted hot, broke away from the Langham, who wanted cold, and the London Sketch Club was born.'[42]

Between 1925 and 1926 Leete was Vice-President, President and a member of the dance committee (Leete-Hodge claimed he was President in 1928, although this appears to be an error of memory). He was also an active member of the Savage Club. He designed invitations, menu cards and other artwork for both organisations, notably for the 'Smoking Conversazione', the meetings for conversation, discussion and gossip usually about art matters, that were so popular at that time.

Members also hosted meetings and parties at their own houses and studios, and the London Sketch Club quickly developed a reputation for its lively parties and diverse entertainments.

Membership was eclectic. A.E. Johnson was a lay member. Robert Baden-Powell was a member, although art was not his primary profession. Other prominent members included the illustrator Edmund Dulac, the mainstream maritime painter Charles Dixon, and the official war artist and former Vorticist C.R.W. Nevinson. Sir George Younger of William Younger's Brewery was also a member, which explains how Leete gained an introduction to that company.[43]

Harry Lawrence Oakley was a longstanding member who was president of the club from 1947 to 1948. He had served with the Green Howards in World War I, and was renowned for his silhouette pictures cut with scissors. He would have contributed to the frieze that ran around the walls of the main drawing room of the club featuring the profiles of members that included Leete. Oakley produced a silhouette of the Prince of Wales (later the Duke of Windsor) and his skills were utilised in several notable recruitment advertisements and posters that were emulated by others in Britain and abroad.

John Hassall was one of the most influential poster artists and teachers of the period. He was known as the 'King of Poster Artists' and he was an influential associate of Leete. In his publication *The London Sketch Club* (Alan Sutton, 1994), David Cuppleditch noted that Hassall 'thrived during the years 1890–1914 when new colour printing processes were being exploited, printers' wages were low and paper was cheap'.

Hassall was born in Walmer, Kent. He had originally turned to fellow county artist, Thomas Sidney Cooper, based in Canterbury, for assistance and guidance. Cooper was renowned for his oil paintings of cows, many of which were exhibited at the Royal Academy of Arts, and he was unimpressed with Hassall's work. However, he was not deterred and, after studying in Antwerp and Paris, Hassall eventually was acknowledged by the art establishment – being elected a member of the Royal Institute of Painters in Water Colours (RI) and the Royal Society of Miniature Painters, Sculptors and Gravers.

In 1900, Hassall opened his own New Art School and School of Poster Design in Kensington, where he numbered Bert Thomas, Bruce Bairnsfather, H.M. Bateman, Harry Rountree and Sidney Strube among his

Across: 'Smoking Conversazione' artwork.
Below: Hassall's work inspired Leete.

students. The school was closed at the outbreak of World War I, however, during the post-war period, he ran the very successful John Hassall Correspondence School.

John Hassall acknowledged Alphonse Mucha, the Czech-born Art Nouveau painter and decorative artist, as a formative influence on his work. Mucha produced many advertisements, designs, illustrations, paintings and postcards that enjoyed enormous popularity in England. The flat colours enclosed by the thick, black lines that featured in these designs became the trademark style of Hassall and contemporaries such as Dudley Hardy, among others.

Hassall is best remembered today for his poster SKEGNESS IS SO BRACING, featuring the Jolly Fisherman skipping along the beach. It was originally commissioned by the Great Northern Railway (GNR) company and first printed by David Allen and Sons (one of the main printers approved by the PRC during World War I) in 1908.[44] Skegness adopted the Jolly Fisherman as its mascot and it is still used today to promote the Lincolnshire seaside resort.

This poster was copied and parodied at the time and continues to attract the attention of modern day cartoonists. Leete produced his own wartime parody, entitled 'The East Coast Is So Bracing – To Recruiting' (which included an acknowledgement to Hassall's poster), for *London Opinion* on 26th December 1914. In Leete's version, the skipping sailor's pipe has fallen out of his mouth, and he turns with a terrified expression as a large gun shell whizzes past him. Leete also created another version inspired by Hassall for the cover of Weston-super-Mare official tourist guides. It depicted a girl holding on to her bonnet and clutching her bucket and spade on the beach, with the slogan 'Atlantic Breezes' (1925).

Hassall and Leete would certainly have been familiar with each other's work. Both were associated with *London Opinion*. Hassall had contributed a cover to the 6th June 1914 issue. Although there is no record of Leete attending Hassall's art school, a stylistic comparison of their work reveals that Leete was undoubtedly influenced by him. Hassall had been elected a member of the London Sketch Club in May 1898 and Leete joined later on 11th December 1914 – proposed by A.E. Horne, Reginald Arkell, Edgar L. Patterson, Harry Rountree and Bert Thomas (prior to this, Leete would have been known to the club as a guest

member). Both Leete and Hassall lived close to each other in west London: Leete at 26, Bedford Gardens, Kensington, and Hassall a short walk away at 88, Kensington Park Road, Notting Hill Gate. As noted earlier, it is likely that Hassall had a hand in the overall design of the David Allen and Sons propaganda poster that featured Leete's Kitchener cartoon. Printed in November 1914, this poster lacked the clarity and directness of the *London Opinion* cartoon cover and poster.

The *London Opinion* artists

Many of Leete's fellow clubmen were also contributors to *London Opinion* and they included William Heath Robinson and two of his proposers who supported his membership to

Across: Harry Lawrence Oakley's 'THINK!' Below left: Poster by Thomas. Below right: Cartoon by Bairnsfather.

"*Well, If you knows of a better 'ole, Go to it.*"

the London Sketch Club – Bert Thomas and Reginald Arkell (who was editor of *Men Only* magazine from the 1930s until 1954, when Paul Raymond purchased it).

Bert Thomas was arguably second in popularity to Leete on *London Opinion* magazine during the war years. He worked for the government producing posters for the War Loans and Savings campaigns during World Wars I and II. Arkell was a scriptwriter and comic novelist and the assistant art editor of *London Opinion* magazine. Leete collaborated with him on several literary projects, including propaganda publications such as *All the Rumours* (Duckworth, 1916) and *The Bosch Book* (Duckworth, 1916). However, Leete's best known publication featured the character Schmidt the Spy, and was initially serialised in *London Opinion*, the first part appearing on 24th October 1914. They were collectively published in *Schmidt the Spy and His Messages to Berlin* (Duckworth, 1916), this time both illustrated and written by Leete. His fictional character later inspired a film.

Leete contributed to wartime cartoon exhibitions in Britain and to several publications that were intended to be sent abroad to amuse the troops at the Front, as well as to influence the Allies. They included *The Passing Show*, published by the House of Odhams. The editor, Comyns Beaumont, wrote in the issue of 12th August 1916, entitled 'The Worries of Wilhelm – A Collection of Humorous and Satirical War Cartoons from the pages of *The Passing Show*', that 'the importance of the cartoon is certainly recognised by the Germans… and quite a considerable time back as the war goes, the Huns, who are totally unable to appreciate shafts of satire when directed against themselves, savagely announced that when they captured London certain editors of offending journals would be hanged for daring to make fun of the sacred person of the Kaiser.' He concluded: 'I may, perhaps, be allowed to claim that both by encouraging our own people, and by flinging these shafts at the Huns, at a time when moral influence is properly regarded as of first-rate importance, the cartoonists whose work appear here are contributing their quota to the world war.'

After the war, Leete produced a very popular book called *A Book of Dragons, Including Many Episodes in the Life of Dennys,*

Schmidt the Spy.

Rouge Dragon of the Fiery Breath (Illustrated London Newspapers, circa 1931). This character inspired the naming of a pub in Weston-super-Mare: The Dragon Inn, owned by J.D. Wetherspoon.

Returning to the war years, it is clear that Leete was conscious of the comic potential of recruitment posters and slogans, as evidenced by his humorous pen and ink wash original artwork for a cartoon produced in 1917, now in the Imperial War Museum, which features the 'Crown Prince Son' saying 'What did you do in the Great War, Daddy?' This derives from Savile Lumley's controversial poster. Lumley was a popular book illustrator, who during his student days studying at the Royal Academy of Arts shared a studio with the cartoonist, illustrator and poster designer George Stampa in St John's Wood.

In *The Street of Ink, an Intimate History of Journalism*, Henry Simonis noted the period when Bert Thomas and Alfred Leete were called up for war service in 1917: 'Bert Thomas, our cartoonist, is building up a reputation. Both he and that versatile genius, Alfred Leete, are just called up for the Army, and we shall miss their splendid work tremendously. Heaven help them if, after their innumerable jests at the expense of the Kaiser and "Little Willie", either of them should be taken prisoner!'

Leete, Thomas and Fred Buchanan, another contributor to *London Opinion*, all joined the Artists Rifles (AR). A photograph of Leete depicts him at Hare Hall (now the Royal Liberty School), within Gidea Park in Essex and where officers were trained, alongside the cartoonists Fred Buchanan and Sidney Strube, who worked for *The Bystander* and later became the political cartoonist of the *Daily Express*. The AR was raised in 1859 as a volunteer light infantry unit. The regiment saw active service during the Boer War and World War I, earning a number of battle honours. Celebrated artists associated have included Ford Maddox Brown, William Holman Hunt, John Everett Millias, Dante Gabriel Rossetti, Lord Leighton, the cartoonists and illustrators Charles Keene and John Leech, along with 'Fougasse' and John and Paul Nash.

The Artists Rifles Regimental Association (ARRA) was inaugurated at a mass meeting of all artists available on 29th June 1916, at the 2nd Battalion's headquarters at Gidea Park. In *A History of The Artists Rifles, 1859–1947* (Pen and Sword, 2006), Barry Gregory explained that as Leete was medically unfit for a commission in 1917 he served as a company clerk with the 2nd Battalion. As a cartoonist and illustrator, he was often in demand by the regiment during and after the war to illustrate dinner menus and memorabilia for regimental occasions.

The ARRA published a magazine that was distributed to all members of the regiment in France and England, where it was offered for sale on bookstalls. Along with Leete, it featured contributions from Fred Buchanan, C.H. Bretherton, Tom Purvis, S.C. 'George' Strube, Bert Thomas, R.F.W. Rees and many others. *The Times* was kind enough to say that 'the *Artists Rifles' Journal* is the best Regimental publication yet produced', whilst the *Daily Telegraph* said: 'This is the best soldiers' paper we have yet seen.'

Without a doubt though, Leete's most significant contribution to the war effort was his cartoon of Kitchener. Leete would have been surprised at how his artwork for *London Opinion* was adapted within the British Empire and by the Allies during the war, and later by Britain's former enemies too.

Your King and Country Need
YOU!

Come and Enlist with the
QUEBEC RIFLES

171st Overseas Battalion
C. E. F.

**Someone is waiting for you at Headquarters
72½ St. Peter Street or Y. M. C. A. Barracks**

L'Association Civile de Recrutement
du District de Québec

CHAPTER 4

THE INFLUENCE OF 'YOUR COUNTRY NEEDS YOU'

IN AUSTRALIA, CANADA, INDIA, NEW ZEALAND AND SOUTH AFRICA

BRITAIN DID EXPORT recruitment posters to individual member states and dominions of the Empire during World War I, but most of them also produced their own posters. Some specified that designs should capitalise on their own national characteristics and particular needs. The face of Lord Kitchener would have limited effectiveness in certain countries, such as India and the USA, whilst in others it was necessary to incorporate imagery and wording into poster designs that had meaning and significance to specific ethnic groups.

Canada

The curators of the McGill University collection of recruitment posters in Canada have

identified that 'the imagery of [our] posters was, both thematically and graphically, similar to that of British war posters and this was largely because of the imperial and constitutional ties between Canada and Britain'.

Ethnic groups within Canada, and for that matter across the British Empire, had to be targeted in a different way, with imagery and slogans in various languages or dialects that had meaning to each group. A poster that came across as being too 'English' in tone and subject was not going to work well among French-Canadians, Irish-Canadians (see poster, on page 101), Jewish-Canadians (see poster, left) and Canadians of Scottish descent.

Some British posters, however, were directly translated from English into French. Like British posters, their Canadian counterparts avoided graphic horror images of war. The major printing centres producing posters were in the cities of Hamilton, Montreal and Toronto.[45]

Printed in Montreal in 1915, the poster entitled 'Let his heart a thousandfold Take the field again!' ARE YOU ONE OF KITCHENER'S OWN? is clearly an adaptation of Leete's KITCHENER design.

Another example, created by an anonymous designer in circa 1917–1918, had the slogan 'You Are Needed To Take My Place – Go With "Kitchener's Own" The 244th Batt.' It showed a soldier standing with his left arm in a sling and right arm outstretched with hand pointing, evoking Leete's LORD KITCHENER design. The poster was published by The Mortimer Co. Ltd., in Montreal, Quebec (see the illustration in the introduction).

A third poster (see poster on page 100), by an unknown designer, entitled SOUSCRIVEZ A L'EMPRUNT DE LA "VICTOIRE" ('Subscribe to

Souscrivez à
L'Emprunt de la "Victoire"

the Victory Loan') and issued in circa 1917 by the Victory Bond Committee, Ottawa, also derived from Leete's cartoon although it depicted a soldier with an outstretched left arm.

Marc H. Choko addressed the subject of print runs of posters in *Canadian War Posters, 1914–1918, 1939–1945* (Canada Communication Group, 1994), noting that both official and private runs ranged from a few hundred to 50,000 copies. Although there was no central government agency controlling the production of all the war posters, the federal government did establish the War Poster Service in 1916. It produced some posters in both English and French. In addition, charities and businesses also printed posters privately.

Choko noted that 'The initiatives were many and varied, coming from companies and from wealthy citizens wishing to participate in the war effort. Recruitment posters were made by individual regiments, which contracted printing companies close to the quarters. The commandant would sometimes ask for price quotations and request adjustments to the graphic design or text. After he paid for and took delivery of the posters, he was then responsible for posting them in appropriate spots.'

He also observed that 'The quality of the posters depended, of course, on the talent of the graphic designers working at the printing companies most of whom were accustomed to creating realistic posters to sell consumer products. Some borrowed directly from foreign works and adapted them to the situation. In some cases, the image was appropriated and reframed and a different text was added.'

In the preface to Choko's publication, Robert R. Fowler wrote: 'I find it amazing that during the Great War of 1914–1918 from a population of about eight million, this country managed to raise an army of over 600,000, a Navy of 9,600 personnel and 115 vessels, and sent more than twenty thousand young men to serve in the British flying services, as well as over 3,000 nursing sisters with the medical corps. What was more shocking was the cost in human lives. The worst example was in the Canadian Expeditionary Corps – the largest active army formation ever to have been organised by Canada – about 60,000 died, a fatality rate of 14.2 per cent (a further 138,166 were wounded). When casualties rose to extreme levels, the government introduced conscription, a move that led to severe unrest and nearly undermined national unity in 1917–18.'

British Parliamentary Recruiting Committee records of letters from Canada praising their recruitment posters

Mr Leicester A. Bonner, Van Winkle, Cariboo, B.C., 28th June 1915

'Thanks very much for your recruiting posters. We had a recruiting rally in Cariboo and got 71 and more to go. I did a bit to help in taking the officers round, and they expressed their appreciation of the posters.'

Mr W.H. Danby, Victoria Gas Co., Ltd., Victoria, B.C., 14th June 1915

'The posters you sent have done a lot of good. You should see the letters of thanks I have received from those to whom I sent them.'

Sir Thomas Tait, Citizens' Recruiting Association, McGill Building, Montreal, 13th March 1915

'The posters issued by your Association have attracted a very great deal of comment on this side of the Atlantic, and there still exists a great demand for them. Even American visitors are continually making applications for them, as they admire them so.'

Mr S.W. Dawson, Travellers Building Sample Rooms, 3rd Avenue, Saskatoon, SASK, 27th August 1915

'Through this advertising matter and Recruiting medium I can trace directly an enlistment of over 30 men.'

Mr W. F. Currie, Box 547, Arcola, Saskatchewan

'I thank you very much for the posters, and I feel sure that they will help us a very great deal in getting recruits as they are, I can assure you, a very great draw here.'

Mr A.O. Huguet, 'the Manse', Wilmer, B.C., 15th October 1915

'It is surprising what an amount of public interest has been awakened by the posters. They have been posted up in the most prominent positions, and they have stirred people.'

The Hon. A.L. Sifton, Premier of Alberta, 17th January 1916

'Yours of the 23rd. December enclosing parcel of British recruiting posters received. I have distributed the various ones received at different times, and I have no doubt that they have been made as useful as possible. This batch is certainly very effective.'

Capt. A.H. Thorburn, Recruiting Officer, C.E.F., Ottawa, 29th November 1915

'We find that the English recruiting posters are much more attractive than any we have been able to secure here.'

Mr Thos. B. Lee, 30, Front Street East, Toronto, 24th December 1915

'The reason I am asking for this particular one ("THE FLAG") is the fact that we have also here in Canada quite a number of Recruiting Posters, but nothing that seems to have caught the eye as much as the one referred to.'

Mr A.H. Abbott, Hon. Sec., Speakers' Patriotic League, University of Toronto, 19th April 1916

'We can assure you that the posters which you have sent have been distributed not merely in our Division but also throughout Canada, and they have done good work.'

Miss M.S. Chase, Kentville, Novia Scotia

'Accept our thanks for your splendid posters. They are doing their work.'

South Africa

In July 1915, South Africa formed the South African Overseas Expeditionary Force (SAOEF) and this force of volunteers was placed under British operational command for activities on the Western Front. Britain still had strong imperial bonds with South Africa

Mr T.J. Holden, Asst. Manager, The Standard, St. Catherines, Ont., 1st September 1915

'Your posters have been of splendid service here in stirring up the enthusiasm of the young men of our city, and recruiting has taken on an added interest.'

Lieut. G.D. Burn, C.O.T.C. 255, Metcalf Street, Ottawa, 6th December 1915

'They (the posters) are so much better than the average Canadian poster that they attract attention more quickly.'

despite the recent protracted Boer Wars against the British Empire that led to independence from Britain.

During the Second Boer War (1899–1902), Louis Botha, the Prime Minister of South Africa during World War I, and Jan Smuts, the Defence Minister, had served as generals. Although both men faced widespread Afrikaner discontent and opposition at home, they were united in their resistance to the German Empire and became prominent members of the British Imperial War Cabinet. In turn, the British government realised that their faces and words were of enormous value (especially Botha) in terms of recruitment, and posters were produced highlighting their military achievements and deeds to help recruit soldiers for the British Empire war.[46]

One poster from the IWM's collections (reference: PST 12329) combined words from Botha with Leete's war cartoon of Kitchener, featured at the top of the poster. It contained the words 'GENERAL BOTHA says: "The South African Brigade in Europe has won a splendid reputation, not alone as fighters, but also as gentlemen. The honour and the name of South Africa have been enhanced and enriched by the heroic deeds of her sons."' It carried the slogan 'South Africans! YOU'RE WANTED – Roll

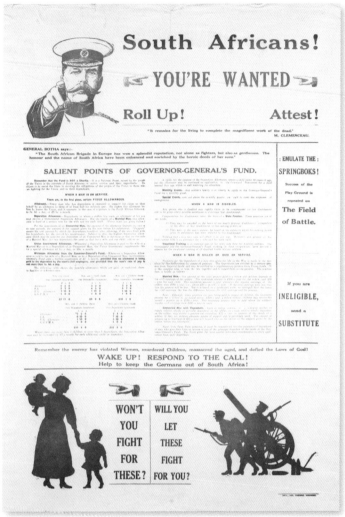

Up! Attest!' It was printed by D.F.A. Ltd. in Kimberley, probably in 1915.

Official South African military records show that, in terms of military contributions and casualties, 'More than 146,000 whites, 83,000 blacks and 2,500 people of mixed race and Asians served in South African military units during the war, in German South-West Africa and 30,000 on the Western Front. An estimated 3,000 South Africans also joined the Royal Flying Corps. The Commonwealth War Graves

commission has records of 9,457 known South African War dead during World War I.'

The co operation of the South African government and the ideal geographical position of the country aided Britain with essential rest stops and safe ports, and provided a strategic advantage in defending her Empire and ensuring that vital sea lanes to the British Raj remained open.[47]

British Parliamentary Recruiting Committee records of letters from South Africa praising their recruitment posters

Messrs. Stuttaford's Stores, Cape Town, 21ˢᵗ August 1915

'Our windows have been posted up with them and they were quite a distinguished feature, as all other posters used were only locally done, and but few designs. The coloured ones were particularly effective. You will probably know that Cape Town has given the lead to South African recruiting, for which, no doubt, your posters have contributed greatly.'

Mr F.W. Cooper, Librarian, Public Library, Port Elizabeth, 17ᵗʰ April 1916

'The posters which you kindly sent us from time to time have been extensively used during the recent recruiting campaign for German East Africa.'

India

Recruitment in India during the British Raj was voluntary. The British Indian Army was the largest of the colonial military forces raised from the native population and led by British officers. It has been estimated that more than 1.5 million men were active during

Above: **Money was a motivator for many** Indian soldiers. **Across:** Gujarati language poster by B.J. Evans: 'Have you bought war bonds or not?'

the war, serving in every major theatre of operations.

Posters were specifically designed to recruit Indian soldiers using images of India. A variant of Leete's Kitchener war cartoon was used for one poster, but not in fact for recruitment – rather, it was to promote the sale of war bonds. An example is now part of the IWM's collections. It was designed by B.J. Evans, circa 1918, and printed in Gujarati, a language widely spoken in India.

Letters sent home by Indian soldiers from the Front provide valuable insights into their thoughts and feelings about the conflict. They knew that their letters were being censored and so they developed ways to circumnavigate the monitoring and censorship. David Omissi, writing about *India and the Western Front* (BBC online history), observed how one soldier wrote home in a coded language, stating that 'the black pepper is very pungent, but only a little remains' – meaning that the Indian troops (black pepper) were fighting very fiercely, but had suffered heavy losses, and implying that enlistment was therefore unwise.

For many Indians there was a strong sense of honouring their clan or caste, and also of personal duty to the Emperor-King George V, far more so than to Lord Kitchener. Although Lord Kitchener had been Commander-in-Chief in India (1902–1909) and had ambitious plans to reorganise and redistribute the army there, he had fallen out with the Viceroy Lord Curzon of Kedleston, who initially supported his appointment. Kitchener lobbied hard to try to become Viceroy of India but was blocked by John Morley, the Secretary of State for India, who threatened resignation if Prime Minister Herbert Asquith intervened. In the absence of his backing, Kitchener was unable to secure the post.

Money was also a motivator for many Indian soldiers. An infantryman was paid a modest eleven rupees per month, however, this still would have represented a very welcome addition to the arduous peasant life familiar to many soldiers. By November 1918 more than 825,000 Indians had enlisted, in addition to those already serving, and official figures indicate that more than 65,000 Indian soldiers died in the war.

Australia

On 4th August 1914, *The Age* newspaper announced that 'The Commonwealth Ministry this afternoon, after a lengthy meeting and consultation with the Governor-General, clearly indicated that Australia was willing to do her share in upholding the Empire.

'The announcement was made by the Prime Minister who said: "The Government has decided in the event of war to place the Australian vessels under the control of the British Admiralty. We have also decided, in the event of war, to hand over to the Imperial Government an expeditionary force of 20,000 men of any suggested composition to any

Across: Another gesture designed to appeal directly to the viewer. Published by John Sands Ltd, Sydney, 1918.
Left: Poster by David Henry Souter, 1917.

destination desired by the home Government, and the cost and despatch and maintenance will be borne by the Commonwealth Government.'"

The commitment and passionate support for Britain was followed by fighting talk, as reported in the *Sydney Morning Herald* on 6th August 1914: 'Germany stands before the world discredited, a breaker of treaties, and an assailant of weaker nations. All this has given Great Britain a dominant place at the very beginning of hostilities. She is thrice armed with a just quarrel, she has gathered her Empire together in such a solid array… and she has vindicated every step she has taken in the path which threatens to run with blood before the end is reached.

'What remains for us is to possess our souls in patience, while making the necessary contributions of time, means and men to carry on. It is our baptism of fire. Australia knows something of the flames of war, but its realities have never been brought so close as they will be in the near future and the discipline will help us to find ourselves. It will test our manhood and womanhood by an immediate local pressure, even though we never hear a shot fired or get a glimpse of the foe.'

As the Australian educationalist and historian Jeremy Sinclair noted: 'the experience of World War I consolidated Australians' pride in themselves, as many saw the new nation bloodied on the battlefield. The emergence of the ANZAC (Australian and New Zealand Army Corps) legend brought ideas of Australian identity into sharper focus, but in many ways the war experience strengthened loyalty to the British Empire. The war opened up deep divisions in Australia, culminating in the bitter debates over conscription in 1916 and 1917.'[48]

Lord Kitchener had visited Australia before the war in 1910 to recommend a new scheme of military training based on conscription. Conscription, however, was an emotive subject in a country with a strong Irish Catholic population and with a union movement concerned about the importation of cheap foreign workers if conscription was introduced. However, the two referenda of 1916 and 1917 were both defeated, and as the records of the National Archives of Australia succinctly summarised: 'The conscription referenda were divisive politically, socially and within religious circles. Newspapers and magazines of the time demonstrate the concerns, arguments, and the passion of Australians in debating this issue. The decisive defeat of the second referendum closed the issue of conscription for the remainder of the war.'

The Australian Imperial Force was a volunteer force formed on 15th August 1914, shortly after the declaration of war. Strictly speaking, the First Australian Imperial Force (1st AIF) was the main expeditionary force during World War I and it was generally known at the time as the AIF. Today, it is referred to as the 1st AIF to distinguish it from the 2nd AIF, which was raised during World War II. The 1st AIF included the Australian Flying Corps, which was later renamed the Royal Australian Air Force.

The Imperial War Museum contains a striking circular poster design (IWM reference: PST 16572) that features Winston Churchill in place of Kitchener. Churchill's outstretched arm and pointing finger are accompanied with the slogan 'Your Country Needs YOU!' Join the A.I.F NOW!' Judging from the age and appearance of Churchill, this was certainly issued during World War II. However, another adaptation closer to Leete's LORD KITCHENER design was printed in Australia during World War I. It was simply entitled CARRY ON! An example printed by S.T.L. between 1915 and 1918 can be found in the IWM's collections and in the National Library of Australia in Canberra.

The arrival of British recruitment posters was recorded in South Australia in the Adelaide newspaper *The Register*, which noted on 9th April 1915: 'A cable message was published on Thursday announcing that Earl Kitchener was calling for more men for the front. In view of this appeal it was interesting to peruse a set of recruiting posters from England, which were exhibited in the window of Messrs. Crawford & Co.'s premises in King William Street. Mr R.H. Crawford received the sheets by the latest mail from England.

Above: An Australian adaptation of Leete's famous Kitchener cartoon.

Across: A circular AIF poster featuring Churchill.

'One of the posters bears the drawing of a bugler in full uniform. It is inscribed: "Another call. More men and still more men, until the enemy is crushed". A second paper is adorned with a picture of a member of an advance guard spying out the land. It urges: "Britons! Your country wants you". [A similar slogan to the *London Opinion* BRITONS – WANTS YOU poster, although in this instance a different design.] An additional notice asks: "What have you done for your Empire? Now is your chance to show what you can do". A poster, which should especially appeal to Australians, says, "Be a sportsman, and lend a hand to the

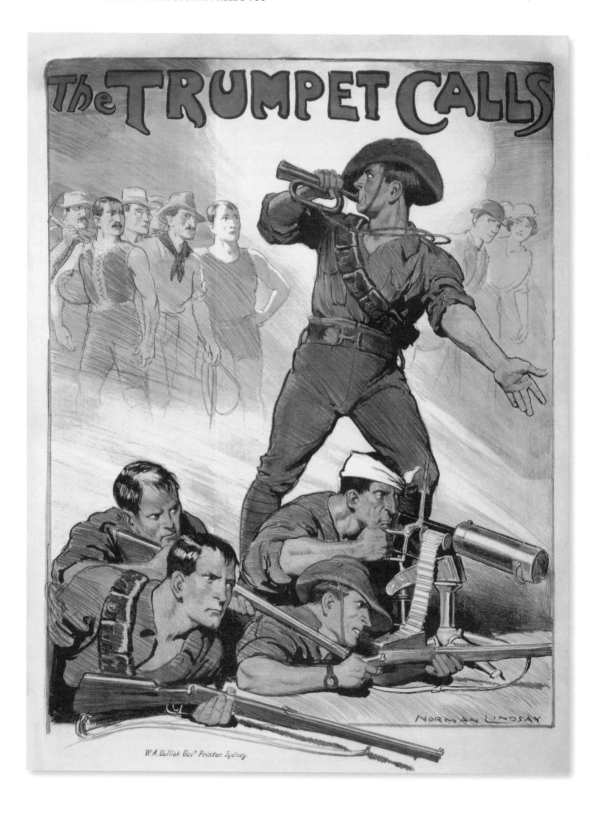

lads at the front. They want your help." Those who cannot go to the war are advised in one placard: "If you can't join the army yourself, get a recruit."'

From mid-June 1915, there was a substantial increase in Australian recruitment. The recruitment drive was put together in a similar manner to that in Britain. Posters were commissioned by the Federal Parliamentary War Committee (then headquartered in Melbourne) and individual states also produced their own posters. In June 1915, the Minister for Defence set recruitment goals at 5,300 men per month in order to maintain the forces fighting at Gallipoli. Although British posters – the PRC designs that could be spared – were exported to Australia, there was a preference arguably forced upon them to adapt the best British ones, or produce their own designs.

The motivations for Australians enlisting were multilayered. Their enthusiasm was due to a sense of adventure, well-paid exotic travel (at five shillings a day for those serving overseas, it was the highest wage of any army at the time) and comradeship combined with machismo and patriotic feelings towards Britain.

The love of outdoor pursuits, riding and sports generated many memorable recruitment posters of the period.[49] Among the leading exponents of Australian propaganda poster design – and the most controversial – was Norman Lindsay (1879–1969). He outlined his commitment to the government and his support of the propaganda effort in his autobiography *My Mask* (Angus and Robertson, 1970) in which he revealed that he 'handed [his] services over to propaganda whenever it was required of [him]'.

Lindsay's controversial 'German Monster', and across, his stirring 'The Trumpet Calls' poster.

Lindsay's THE TRUMPET CALLS was produced by William Gullick, the government printer based in Sydney, New South Wales, on behalf of the Australian Commonwealth Government in 1915. According to Museum Victoria in Melbourne this was a popular poster 'depicting a soldier in khaki with a bugle to his mouth, looking urgently over his right shoulder. Four soldiers lie beneath him, each aiming a firearm. One has a bandaged head. Behind the bugler appear shadowy figures of civilians, including a stockman, surfer, labourer in leather jerkin, and a well-dressed middle-class couple.'

Six of Lindsay's posters were intended to be posted at various stages in the last few months of 1918. The first was GERMAN MONSTER, which was secretly posted overnight in October. This poster retains the power to shock today through the image of a bestial figure with its bloodstained hands grasping a globe, representing German militarism. Its contentious nature raised questions in the Federal Parliament. Lindsay is likely to have been inspired by H.R. Hopps' brutal American poster of 1917, captioned 'Destroy This Mad Brute – Enlist'. It depicted a moustachioed ape-like monster wearing the German soldier's spiked helmet (the *pickelhaube* worn at the beginning of the war) and carrying a bloodstained club, marked '*Kultur*', in his right hand and a dishevelled woman over his left arm.

Lindsay's GERMAN MONSTER was followed by three posters: QUICK!; GOD BLESS DEAR DADDY WHO IS FIGHTING THE HUN AND SEND HIM HELP; as well as WILL YOU FIGHT NOW OR WAIT FOR THIS, which portrayed the German enemy as a brutal barbarian and violator. However, according to some sources, another

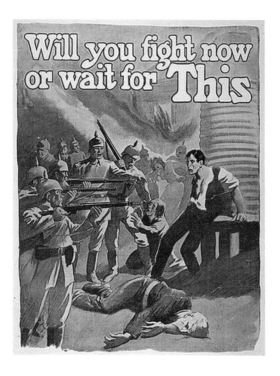

Posters by Troedel & Cooper (above); Lindsay, 1917 (left); unknown artist, 1917 (opposite top); and A. Vaughan [an Adelaide printer], 1915, an adaptation of PRC poster No. 82 (opposite below).

two designs – THE LAST CALL and FALL-IN! (the latter poster depicted smiling soldiers marching) – were printed but were deemed not suitable for public display.[50]

Lindsay was born in Creswick, Victoria, and is widely regarded as one of Australia's greatest artists. His former home at Faulconbridge, New South Wales, is now the Norman Lindsay Gallery and Museum. In addition to painting, he practised as a cartoonist, sculptor and writer. He also boxed.

Boxing was popular in Australia and it was a useful skill in battle. One popular recruitment poster published in 1917 by the State Parliamentary Recruiting Committee, depicted

Lieutenant Albert Jacka, VC, as a role model for a huge campaign to enlist sportsmen into the Australian Imperial Force. Jacka achieved instant fame back home when he became the first Australian to win the Victoria Cross during World War I, on 19th July 1915. According to information from the Australian War Memorial records, it was said that one of the reasons he was such a good soldier, and had such a fighting attitude 'was that he had been a boxer before the war. The campaign to enlist sportsmen was fuelled by a strong belief that by playing sport young men developed specific skills and qualities that could be used on the battlefield.'

An adaptation of Leete's KITCHENER design was printed in 1917 by Troedel & Cooper in Melbourne, and had the slogan 'Which? MAN You Are Wanted! In The Sportsmen's 1000'. To the upper left of the poster is a picture of a

military medal and to the right are images of sports equipment.

Another variant was produced by the Tasmanian-born architect, artist, cartoonist and illustrator Harry John Weston (1874–1955). Entitled U ARE WANTED IN THE SPORT'S UNIT, and printed by Stewart Black Lithographers, Sydney, it was published by the Sportsmen's Recruiting Committee in 1917 and featured the pointing finger of an Australian soldier. It was inspired both by Leete's Kitchener cartoon and PRC poster number 125 WHO'S ABSENT? IS IT YOU?, a design that was also a Leete variant and replaced Lord Kitchener with John Bull. This last named poster was sent to Australia and one can still be seen as part of the official Australian war records in the National Archives, Canberra.

The statistics for Australian participation in World War I are bewildering. On

the eve of war, Australia had a population of 4.9 million, but 416,809 Australian soldiers enlisted, including more than 400 indigenous Australians, with 331,000 men serving overseas. By the end of the war, 61,966 Australian servicemen had died.

New Zealand

The New Zealand Expeditionary Force of soldiers fought with Australia as the Australian and New Zealand Army Corps (ANZAC) at Gallipoli. Additional New Zealand forces also served in Palestine and on the Western Front.

A collection of around 130 recruiting posters now forms part of the Museum of New Zealand/ Te Papa Tongarewa, in Wellington. Originally part of a larger group, the posters were acquired

towards the end of and immediately after the war – for an intended national war museum in Wellington that was never built. The posters were subsequently donated to various collections, and an excellent article by Stephanie Gibson, one of the curators, examined in detail how they were acquired and the reception of the posters at the time. At the time of writing, her article can be found on the museum's website.

Gibson emphasised that New Zealand's advertising industry during the war was relatively undeveloped and the Government Printing Office was depleted of staff, as they were serving in the war. So, for pragmatic and economic reasons, the government was reliant on donations of PRC posters from Britain, as well as purchasing designs from Australia.

Among the photographs of recruiting stations in New Zealand, one of the Auckland station on 23rd April 1917 stands out clearly as a vivid example of which posters were favoured for public display. It was photographed by Henry Winkelmann and is part of the Sir George Grey Special Collections, Auckland Libraries. It reveals the array of British posters affixed to the recruitment building and above the porch, including: It's Our Flag, designed by Guy Lipscombe; and Take Up The Sword of Justice, by Bernard Partridge. Between them is a poster entitled Come Lads Give us a spell by Annie J. Hope Campbell, which was published by the Victoria State Parliamentary Recruiting Committee, Australia, in 1915. It depicted soldiers within a Gallipoli-like landscape'. There is no sign of the Britons – Wants YOU poster, or the David Allen and Sons variant. Gibson noted that as the photograph was taken in April 1917 the posters displayed must have been there for many months as conscription had been introduced in 1916.

Within the collections of the Imperial War Museum in London there is a New Zealand poster depicting a giant hand with pointing finger that is clearly an adaptation of Leete's Lord Kitchener cartoon. It is entitled YOU BE IN THE 3ᴿᴰ LIBERTY LOAN – £35,000,000 (IWM reference: PST 16810), but it was produced during World War II. However, the slogan 'Your Country Needs YOU' was actively used during World War I in various New Zealand newspapers – notably in the *Feilding Star*, *Ohinemuri Gazette* and *Wanganui Chronicle*, among others.

Around 100,000 New Zealand troops and medical personnel served overseas throughout the war, excluding those in British and other Dominion forces, from a population of just over a million. The casualties in terms of injuries and deaths were incredibly high, one of the highest of the war per capita, with more than 18,000 killed and 41,317 wounded.[51]

British Parliamentary Recruiting Committee records of letters from Australia and New Zealand praising their recruitment posters

The Librarian, Parliament Library, Melbourne
  'I am in receipt of your letter of the 1st ult., together with the fine recruiting poster enclosed. I have displayed it in a prominent place in the Library.'

Mr M. Marks, 250, Wellington Street, Collingwood, Victoria, 21ˢᵗ June 1915
  'Your posters are serving their purpose in a most pronounced manner, as since their display the number of those enlisting has considerably increased.'

The Auckland City Recruiting Centre Station, 23ʳᵈ April 1917. Across: 'It's Our Flag' (visible also in the scene above).

Gordon Sprigg, Royal Colonial Institute, Northumberland Avenue, W.C., 3ʳᵈ September, 1915
  'Your posters have aroused a tremendous amount of enthusiasm and have given great impetus to recruiting in the states of the Australian Commonwealth.'

Rev. E.H. Stammer, St. John's Vicarage, Uralla, N.S.W. [no date given]
  'The packet of recruiting posters you forwarded at the end of July duly arrived, and have done their little bit towards stimulating recruits. They are very effective indeed.'

Sergt. R. Mc. C. Sprott, Napier Troop, Legion of Frontiersman, Port Ahuriri, Napier, N.Z., 6ᵗʰ December 1915
  'Please accept our very best thanks for the very fine posters you so kindly forwarded me. I had them mounted on calico and rollers and varnished, so that they will last for some time in open weather, and distributed them to the very best advantage.'